Pi

1

GW01551310

TERI KING'S
ASTROLOGICAL HOROSCOPES
FOR 1995

Pisces

**Teri King's complete horoscope
for all those whose birthdays
fall between
20 February and 20 March**

ELEMENT
Shaftesbury, Dorset ● Rockport, Massachusetts
Brisbane, Queensland

© Teri King 1994

Published in Great Britain in 1994 by
Element Books Limited
Longmead, Shaftesbury, Dorset

Published in the USA in 1994 by
Element, Inc
42 Broadway, Rockport, MA 01966

Published in Australia in 1994 by
Element Books Limited for
Jacaranda Wiley Limited
33 Park Road, Milton, Brisbane, 4064

Cover design by Max Fairbrother
Design by Roger Lightfoot
Typeset by The Electronic Book Factory Ltd, Fife
Printed and bound in Great Britain by
BPC Paperbacks Ltd, Aylesbury, Bucks

British Library Cataloguing in Publication
data available

Library of Congress Cataloging in Publication
data available

ISBN 1–85230–517–7

Element Books regrets that it cannot enter into any
correspondence with readers requesting information
about their horoscope.

Contents

Contents

Introduction

Astrology has many uses, not least of these its ability to help us to understand both ourselves and other people. Unfortunately there are many misconceptions and confusions associated with it, such as that old chestnut – how can the zodiac forecast be accurate for all the millions of people born under one particular sign?

The answer to this is that all horoscopes published in newspapers, books and magazines are, of necessity, of a general nature. Unless an astrologer can work from the date, time and place of your birth, the reading given will only be true for the typical member of your sign.

For instance, let's take a person born on 9 August. This person is principally a subject of Leo, simply because the Sun occupied that section of the heavens known as Leo during 24 July to 23 August. However, when delving into astrology at its most serious, there are other influences which need to be taken into consideration. For example, the Moon. This planet enters a fresh sign every 48 hours. On the birth date in question it may have been in, say, Virgo. And if this were the case it would make our particular subject Leo (Sun representing willpower) and Virgo (Moon representing instincts) or if you will a Leo/Virgo. Then again the rising sign or 'ascendant' must also be taken into consideration. This also changes constantly as the earth revolves: approximately every two hours a new section of the heavens comes into view – a new sign passes over the horizon. The rising sign is of the utmost importance, determining the image projected by the subject to the outside world – in effect, the personality.

The time of birth is essential when compiling a birth chart. Let us suppose that in this particular instance Leo was rising at the time of birth. Now, because two of the three main influences are Leo, our sample case would be fairly typical of his/her sign, possessing all the faults and attributes associated with it. However, if on the other hand, the Moon and ascendant had been in Virgo then, whilst our subject would certainly display some of the Leo attributes or faults, it is more than likely that for the most part he/she would feel and behave more like a Virgoan.

As if life weren't complicated enough, this procedure must be carried through to take into account all the remaining planets. The position and signs of Mercury, Venus, Mars, Jupiter, Saturn, Uranus, Neptune and Pluto must all be discovered, plus the aspect formed from one planet to another. The calculation and interpretation of these movements by an astrologer will then produce an individual birth chart.

Because the heavens are constantly changing, people with identical charts are a very rare occurrence. Although it is not inconceivable that it could happen, this would mean that the two subjects were born not only on the same date and at the same time, but also in the same place. Should such an incident occur, then the deciding factors as to how these individuals would differ in their approach to life, love, career, financial prospects and so on would be due to environmental and parental influence.

Returning to our hypothetical Leo: our example with the rising Sun in Leo and Moon in Virgo may find it useful not only to read up on his or her Sun sign (Leo) but also to read the section dealing with Virgo (the Moon). Nevertheless, this does not invalidate Sun sign astrology. This is because of the great power the Sun possesses, and on any chart this planet plays an important role.

Belief in astrology does not necessarily mean believing in totally determined lives, that we are predestined and have no control over our fate. But what it does clearly show is that our lives run in cycles, for both good and bad and, with the aid of astrology, we can make the most of, or minimize, certain patterns and tendencies. How this is done is entirely up to the individual. For example, if you are in possession of the knowledge that you are about to experience a lucky few days or weeks, then you can make the most of them by pushing ahead with plans. You can also be better prepared for illness, misfortune, romantic upset and every adversity.

Astrology should be used as it was originally intended – as a guide, especially to character. In this direction it is invaluable and it can help us in all aspects of friendship, work and romance. It makes it easier for us to see ourselves as we really are and, what's more, as others see us. We can recognize both our own weaknesses and strengths and those of others. It can give us both outer confidence, and inner peace.

In the following pages you will find: personality profiles; an in-depth look at the year ahead from all possible angles including numerology; monthly and daily guides; plus, and it is a big plus, information for those poor and confused creatures so often ignored who are born on 'the cusp' – at the beginning or the end of each sign.

Used wisely, astrology can help you through life. It is not intended to encourage complacency, since in the final analysis what you do with your life is up to you. This book will aid you in adopting the correct attitude to the year ahead and thus maximizing your chances of success. Positive thinking is encouraged because this helps us to attract positive situations. Allow astrology to walk hand in hand with you and you will be increasing your chances of success and happiness.

A Fresh Look at Your Sun Sign

As a rule, members of the general public appreciate and understand that for practical reasons Sun sign astrology is fairly general, and therefore for a more in-depth study it is necessary to hire an astrologer who will then proceed to study the date, year, place and time of birth of an individual. Then, by correlating the birth chart with the positions of the different planets, a picture can be slowly drawn for the client.

However, there is also a middle way, which can be illuminating. Each sign comprises 30 'degrees' (or days) and, by reducing these down into three sections, it becomes possible to draw up a picture of each sign which is far more intimate than the usual methods. Therefore, check out your date of birth and draw your own conclusions from the information below.

PISCES (20 February to 20 March)

BORN BETWEEN 20 FEBRUARY AND 1 MARCH

Your Sun falls in the first section of Pisces. Because of this you are a stereotype romantic who enjoys attempting to turn life into poetry in motion. You dwell on plans, dreams, self-induced drama and schemes. You are highly emotional, sentimental, wistful, and occasionally melancholic. Certainly, you are artistic and creative and invariably over-active. Doggedly you look for fantasies come true, divine highs and stimulating romantic situations. Further, when confused you need solitude in order to sort out your more troubled feelings.

Generally speaking, the situations or reasons that induce your temporary gloom seem elusive and hazy, and quite often so is your state of mind. The emotional confusion frequently results in reclusive tendencies, and there are even days when you just cannot be bothered to stir yourself and get out of bed – usually because you simply don't want to. You then allow yourself to drift into a nostalgic or maudlin mood, and this is a temptation you should consciously strive to avoid. Once this mood strikes, you attempt to create an insulating cocoon around yourself in which you can ruminate, withdraw and analyse your emotions. However, despite this need to allow passiveness to take over, you usually have more internal resources at your finger tips than most people. Fundamentally, the problem is that often you simply don't know how to utilize them and they are left untended or ignored.

There is a strong likelihood that you possess psychic ability, an inventive and original mind and tremendous creative talent, all of which could flourish in occult study.

Basically the problem you wrestle with is that your emotions often cripple you to the point where you are too afraid to carry out your own deep desires. It is necessary to think positively and make strenuous efforts to rise above the inclination to put yourself down and hold yourself back. When you have accomplished this you will find that it is far easier to make life a pleasure rather than a problem. But before this can be achieved you must decide that you are more interested in having a go at life than in giving up and passively allowing yourself to be consumed by dissatisfying situations.

BORN BETWEEN 2 MARCH AND 11 MARCH

Your Sun falls in the second section of Pisces. This means that you are more changeable, emotionally sensitive and impressionable than Pisces subjects born in the other sections. Furthermore, you are also more considerate, caring and imaginative. Despite a clear inclination to be idealistic, you also have within your power the means for making your dreams materialize. You are intelligent, intuitive and tenacious, and struggle to overcome negative emotional moods.

Nevertheless, mood swings and changes can undermine your self-confidence and feelings of self-worth, and because of this you should fight hard towards greater emotional balance and self-discipline. Deep within the reaches of your soul is a conflict between your attempts to make your practical ideas materialize and an inclination towards inaction.

Although you have a completely original mind, your dreamy-eyed moods can sometimes prevent progress and keep your plans in a state of dormancy. You possess a tremendous sense of timing but your inclination to wait things out frequently restricts and retards the ultimate results.

As a rule you have a deep enjoyment of life's more sensual pleasures, plus an optimistic approach to life. When driven to extremity, your sybaritic sensibilities usually result in more trouble than you care to consider. It is therefore important that you learn to balance pragmatism with your impressionability or you are likely to become a victim of your own desires.

Once you have managed to discover the middle way between cool, lucid logic and heated inspiration, you will have the golden key to success at your disposal.

BORN BETWEEN 12 MARCH AND 20 MARCH

Your Sun falls in the third section of Pisces. This is an extremely powerful section of your sign because it is associated with change and rebirth. More than likely you carry around with you a heavy karma from which you need to free yourself through the use of spiritual forces. There is an inclination for you to allow painful memories to pull you back into the past. Nevertheless, it is imperative that you re-experience these memories just long enough to resolve them and then free yourself of them for ever.

Luckily you are aware of the fact that new cycles of experience lie ahead. But before you can live life to the fullest extent, you must eliminate the dross which permeates your head and your life. This section is usually deeply aware of change at its most profound – on either a physical or psychological level. There is a strong possibility that you have undergone many serious changes in life, and such upheavals may have appeared more often than you could comfortably cope with. Nevertheless, on each occasion you have overcome your pain through the power within you.

It is likely that you will experience a great deal before you are ready to progress in life. Some of these experiences will be difficult to handle because invariably they will bring about some kind of loss. However, once you have pushed yourself into understanding the higher levels of consciousness you will be able to feel instinctively that what you are losing is only a negative experience or situation that threatens to imprison you unless you can eliminate it from your life.

Should you attempt to resist the natural changes in your life and prefer instead to cling to past memories, relationships and habits that only hamper your ability to grow, you will be creating unnecessary trouble for yourself. You must accept that at some point in life all such experiences will evaporate, whether you like it or not. Provided you are able to use each experience positively, firstly by becoming more self-aware and, secondly, by recognizing your spiritual awareness, you will be moving towards the cycle of freedom illustrated in your following sign, Aries. The sign of the ram represents new beginnings created by self-directed will-power: an unchained will that is free to make the changes that are necessary in order to realize one' full potential.

Crucial to this section is the idea of sacrifice. It is therefore important that you willingly sacrifice your old, negative life patterns before new, constructive ones can form. Should you be unwilling to do this, you will be allowing past experiences to pull you down.

You have the capability to develop a tremendous amount of psychic power. If you are willing to do so you can grasp the highest power it is possible to possess.

WHEN YOU ARE BAD YOU ARE VERY VERY BAD (<u>Horrorscopes</u>)

You seem to be perennially into stress, a person who rarely tires of dramatizing life. Friends become exhausted with the constant repetition of your difficulties. And despite your repeated mistakes you never seem to learn from them. You have an aggressive/passive character that expresses anger in the most complicated way: hysteria, hypochondria, sulking and sarcasm all are utilized, despite the fact that they rarely get you anywhere.

There is an inclination to hole up in a corner and, like a hurt animal, lick your wounds in the hope that others

are watching. But since this is hardly the most effective
attention-getting method, you invariably end up sitting
by yourself feeling abandoned and neglected.

You often allow yourself to become consumed by
situations and people that have a negative effect on
you – and drowning in self-created unhappiness. It is
on these occasions that you roll over, weep your heart
out and play the loser.

For reasons that others find difficult to understand
you find a certain sensationalism in sadness. You allow
yourself to be overcome by sentimentality and are easily
moved by melancholia. It is hardly surprising that your
idea of love is nothing short of a grand finale that
comes complete with enchantment: a package deal, if
you like.

Because of your emotional immaturity, too frequently
you become involved with the wrong people. Your
partners are often married, irresponsible and incapable
of commitment. However, for reasons that only you
understand, you are able to convince yourself that you
can rehabilitate these hopeless cases. Subconsciously,
these problem people help you to keep your distance
and aid you in avoiding too much intimate contact.
Regardless of this, you are not phased: you are able
to take on board whatever you want and rarely listen
to anybody, anyway. The fantasy side to your character
is so ingrained that often you don't really need a mate
– a mental trip is quite satisfactory. Your involvement
with reality is so remote that it is an easy matter for
you to avoid confronting anything you don't wish to.
However, once you isolate yourself from what is going
on in your life, you start to feel alienated, lonely and
depressed.

Conversely, you are possessive about such mood
swings, morose moments and depressions. You think
you need solitude, not helpful advice. And even if you

were given any it is unlikely that you would listen or show any gratitude. Invariably you prefer to hide rather than confront the world, just like a coward. Basically, you have little idea of what you really want, although you certainly make a fuss when you can't have it. Unless you face up to your own passiveness and stop complaining and analysing yourself, you will never be free from a permanent anxiety attack.

You may even prefer to live your life as a victim. If you do then bear in mind that you really are your own worst enemy – no one in your life could possibly play the role as well as you do.

CUSP CASES

PISCES/AQUARIUS CUSP: FEBRUARY 17-22

You may possibly be aware that this is one of the most talented cusps in the Zodiac. This is because you are given the creative artistry of Pisces, plus the vision of Aquarius – a fascinating blend of objectivity and sensitivity. There is a strong possibility that you will be highly original, possibly psychic, and adventurous. When Neptune and Uranus are combined in this way you can accomplish the majority of your ambitions and objectives.

Your creativity is likely to incline you to music, poetry or the artistic world. Possibly you will experience several marriages or long relationships before you are able to locate that special someone who is able to understand you both emotionally and mentally.

PISCES/ARIES CUSP: MARCH 18-23

This cusp contains an interesting blend of the driving, aggressive force of Mars and the inventive visions of Neptune. Because of this you will never be content to simply dream your life away. The Aries side of your character fills you with determination and will certainly boost your Piscean confidence. On the other hand, your Piscean sympathies and consideration will temper the Aries ego.

There is a strong possibility that you are a charming individual with a theatrical inclination, blending positive and negative in a way which is hard for other people to pin down. You can be energetic, mystical and easygoing, and are, in truth, everybody's ideal mate.

The Year Ahead: Overview

As a Piscean, no doubt you often get the distinct impression that you are caught between two worlds – and clearly you experience certain difficulties in coping with this. Frequently you are unsure which is real: the clear substance of everyday life or the realm of your own imagination, which all too often appears to make reality more meaningful.

If you are confused, try hard to imagine how those closest to you feel in their attempts to understand you. You have to acknowledge the fact that you are hard to follow, even on your more illuminating days. When somebody close to you makes an effort to scrutinize your personality, you change under their very gaze. This is because you are a master of disguise and, providing you have a mask to hide behind, you are free to play any role which suits your audience. The question is who is the real you? The chances are the rest of us will never know. This is basically due to the fact that you constantly change your outer persona, involve yourself in over-dramatizing life and are rarely seen without your mask.

How, then, are you likely to react to the coming of a new year? The answer to this question is that secretly you hold high expectations that this year will provide you with an opportunity to shine. The best advice you can take on board is that 1995 will present you with chances to learn various lessons, and provided you can accept this, it will be a period of growth.

From January through to the end of July the stars suggest that you have learnt how to establish yourself and relate to your immediate environment as well as adapt your attitude to everyone and everything close to you, such as relatives and neighbours. You are now able to use these relationships in education, travel and anything that promotes communication. It is likely, too, that you have been developing your mental powers. During this period, you need to learn how to use these powers to deploy resources acquired as a result of contact with other people. Widen your circle of relationships and strive to increase your perceptions, which with any luck will bring revelations, wider vision and inspiration. Higher education and prolonged travel will be especially useful when it comes to broadening and developing your mind.

From August through to the end of the year, it will be apparent that you have learnt how to establish yourself on all levels, mentally, spiritually and emotionally as well as physically. You may also have experienced some hard knocks on the financial front, and this has helped to create a wiser you. For the remainder of the year, you should concentrate on developing an ability to perpetuate your relationships, which you will quickly discover is a real source of power. Furthermore, work on your attitude towards other people's resources and realize that although they may not be yours, they certainly cannot be wasted.

Throughout the year, that planet of upheaval, Pluto, is attempting to free itself from the sign of Scorpio. However, it will remain there for most of January, and from April through to October. During these months you can expect a certain amount of drastic changes in connection with foreign affairs, travel and legal matters. On the positive side, it is likely that Pluto is attempting to sweep away negative influences that have been holding you back for some time now.

At the end of the year Pluto will begin its journey through the sign of Sagittarius, which is at the zenith of your chart. There may follow a period during which you develop a vital need for independence, and even power. You will indeed become more independent, and this can be no bad thing. You will also find it easier to mobilize support from other people. However, there may be some unforeseen twists in your career, although these must be taken in your stride. Pluto will be acting as a new broom, sweeping aside past ambitions and preparing the way for a more prosperous professional future. Providing you do not attempt to stem the tide of events, but can coast along with them, you should experience little difficulty. But it is only those born during the first couple of days of the Piscean period who will be affected in this way during this particular year.

As Pluto begins to traverse Sagittarius and for several years to come, we can all expect a world which will be much improved. Fights will cease between Black and White, Jew and Muslim, and age-old rivalries between men and women will be breached. There are likely to be startling medical breakthroughs, and diseases which now plague the earth will either be prevented or completely cured. Man will become more aware and active in caring and nurturing for mother earth, which he has long polluted. Certainly, Pisces, you have a great deal to look forward to.

Throughout the year Neptune will continue to wend its way through Capricorn. If you were born during the last week of the Pisces period you are likely to become more idealistic and will certainly be making great demands of your friends. Further, you will develop a wide circle of artistic and intuitive contacts and may be highly influenced by them.

Like Pluto, Uranus is also struggling to free itself from the sign of Capricorn, although it only manages to do so during April and May. During the remaining months, you may well experience original aspirations, advanced ideals and remarkable friendships. There will be a marked tendency towards sudden attractions and repulsions and you may be drawn to unconventional, independent, inventive and, of course, mystical people.

During April and May, when Uranus is squatting in the sign of Aquarius, those born during the first two days of the Piscean period will be highly intuitive, and humanitarian instincts will be strong. Should creativity play an important role in your professional life, these two months will be of great significance to you.

Throughout the entire year Saturn will be traversing your sign. This planet is the zodiac's disciplinarian and is there to teach you certain lessons. Working alongside this planet you will not only grow as an individual but will also reach a greater maturity which will serve you for the remainder of your life. Saturn will aid you to be more serious, reliable, self-controlled and industrious. It will help you develop caution, prudence, and patience. Ambitions will be strong but may not progress at the speed you perhaps had hoped for. Nevertheless, you will become more responsible and in turn a far stronger character.

It is a good idea to recognize one or two of the negative possibilities suggested by the placing of Saturn in Pisces, in order to avoid potential difficulties. After all, prevention is always better than cure. These difficulties, however, are only minor. If you are wise you will pay special attention to dental problems during the early part of the year: failure to do so could create major difficulties later on. Furthermore, ensure that you wrap up against inclement weather as a tendency to catch cold is prevalent when we fall under the influence of this planet. Last but not least, should you insist on clambouring around in high places, when Saturn is in a difficult aspect you may be more prone to falls. For further information refer to the monthly and daily guides. But always remember, the stars impel, but they do not compel. In the end you are the master or mistress of your own fate.

For the entire year, Jupiter will be travelling through the zenith of your chart. It is a wonderful placing and should increase your confidence where professional matters are concerned. You are likely to experience your best year for twelve years and great strides can be made. Certainly, you will possess a great desire for achievement and will mix easily with those who can help you. Success, honour, respect and a rise in life are all within your grasp – all you have to do is believe it. It would be a pity not to derive the maximum out of the year ahead – although over-confidence and extravagance are to be discouraged.

During 1995 you are likely to find it much easier to maintain a positive attitude to life. Your belief in your own abilities will be strong and there will be a touch of magic riding alongside you. This year could be a memorable one and long-treasured for years to come.

Career Year

As a rule you are the type of person who shrinks from competition and rivalry and is attracted to the sea, music and writing – anything, in fact, which allows you to create without pressure. Your gift for interpretation can in many cases take you onto the stage as you can obtain great satisfaction by slipping into another guise. Maximum pleasure is gained when executing this characterization in front of an audience.

You are able to excel anywhere where will-power and rational thought are not essential requirements. You flourish when you can exercise your intuition, sympathy, imagination and creative qualities. You make a splendid poet, actor, spinner of dreams. Because of your desire to take care of the sick, the needy and animals, and your love of the sea, you are often attracted to careers in the navy, social work, the church, the medical profession or, on a more basic level, anything connected with fish, plastic or footware. If, through necessity, you become involved in a rather irksome or dull job, developing your artistic instincts in a spare-time activity will greatly aid your peace of mind.

Saturn within your sign for the entire year will be especially lucky for those who work in the sciences or who are in positions of authority. However, for all Pisceans it is a time when persistent effort and a sense of responsibility can be made to pay off. Avoid the temptation to change course when professional matters seem to be heading for troubled waters. Providing you are able to show some consistency, which this planet is helping you to develop, you can only triumph.

The position of Neptune and Uranus in Capricorn for the majority of the year will help those who work for the state or in administration. These planets will also be useful for Pisceans involved with the medical profession, or charitable institutions and organizations: in fact, anything which exists in order to help other people.

Jupiter so prominently placed in your chart throughout the entire year will help those involved in legal matters, banking or insurance. And a little help from you is sure to point to greater prosperity as well as peace of mind where professional matters are concerned. Seldom will you have been in such a strong position to grab the reins of your life and steer a path straight to the top. Whether you decide to make the most of this period is, of course, entirely up to you. However, opportunities and chances beckon and it is a very negative fish who will allow this excellent year to go to waste. There should be improvement all year round but many of the highlights will occur in March and December.

Should you be self-employed, a freelance worker, or wanting to strike out on your own in any way, shape or form, you will not find it difficult to make contact, influence people and find backing for your projects.

Although this is a splendidly lucky and positive year for all fish, it may be exceptional for those involved in the arts or music. Nevertheless, refuse to be downhearted if this is not the case for now, more than at any other time, you will be given the opportunity to push out into life and expand in a positive way. Avoid the Piscean pitfall of allowing yourself to be influenced or deflected by other people's opinions. Believe me, at this moment in time it is you who instinctively knows what needs to be done in order to find success. All you need to do is want it enough.

For further information on the best times of the year to push ahead, refer to the monthly and daily guides.

Money Year

If you are a typical fish, there is a tendency for money to run through your fingers like sand and as a rule you rarely have any idea just how it has disappeared. You are especially drawn to extravagance on dreary days when you feel abandoned and lonely. In your book, a few highs, regardless of the price, can help to boost your spirits and make it easier to cope with life. Pisces is one of the luxury-minded signs: a bottle of the best champagne can assist you through a miserable night, preferably between silk sheets and an attractive body alongside.

In the main, though, you really do not need a mansion house with servants (although you may occasionally admit that this would be quite a good idea). Fundamentally, what you need is comfort, but often your interpretation of this word can be quite costly and those final little touches can so easily get you into trouble if you are not careful.

Conversely, the spiritual side to the Piscean personality can on occasions lead you into believing that you can make a home out of a blanket and use the sky as your roof. If you are operating on this level, the only thing that concerns you about cash is how quickly you can give it away. However, as it is extremely unlikely that to date you have reached this state of evolution, it might be wise to make a list of your priorities, that is, of course, unless you can afford to pay for a costly whirl of pleasure. Even if this were the case, it would still be a good idea to challenge yourself to find contentment with a little less.

One of the reasons why cash can provide you with some heart-stopping moments is the fact that the planet which rules this area of your life is fiery, aggressive, impatient and sexy Mars. Naturally, as one would expect, this planet travels quickly – and so do you when it comes to spending.

Your best chances of exercising self-control are when this planet of energy and speed is passing through one of the earth signs such as Taurus, Virgo or Capricorn. During these periods of the year you will be more focused and able to think twice before splashing out on unnecessary luxuries. On the other hand, watch out when this same planet is wending its way through some of the fire signs, namely Aries, Leo or Sagittarius, for these are the times when you will spend impulsively without thinking of the consequence.

As Mars wends its way through the water signs, in various phases during the year you will be more inclined to spend when emotionally impassioned. Therefore, take preventative action when Mars is proceeding through Cancer, Scorpio and your own sign of Pisces. It is likely that you will be most indifferent to hard cash, Pisces, when your financial planet is passing through the earth signs of Aquarius, Gemini and Libra.

It is quite obvious that when it comes to cash, as with other areas to life, you are a complex and hard-to-understand individual who is very much influenced by the whim of the moment. Because of this you will find the monthly guides invaluable in aiding you to conserve and exercise self-control. Do not, under any circumstances, use the position of Mars to justify your mad extravagances. As always the stars impel but they do not compel; in the end you are at the helm of your life and cannot shift the responsibility onto other people's shoulders.

Luckily, because you seem to be enjoying a great deal of success on the professional front, it is likely that you will have more money at your disposal. Be sure that you stash some of that nasty green stuff away for the proverbial rainy day when it is sure to bucket down. The fact that you possess a soft cushion should allow you to feel much more confident and in control during the year ahead.

It will be a good idea to spend a little bit of cash on sprucing up your image, particularly where professional matters are concerned, and this is the only excuse you have for dipping into any savings. A presentable persona will aid your progress in a startling and lucky way during the coming year. Fortunately, Saturn will be attempting to teach you greater responsibility, and hopefully the effects of this planet will be felt in the cash area of your life.

Above all else, refrain from justifying your extravagance by fooling yourself into believing it is necessary in order to attract the opposite sex. Always bear in mind that you have a great deal to offer other people and that no matter how hard you may try you simply cannot buy love – but then, of course, the same cannot be said for sex.

With your ability to take on board added responsibility, plus the fact Lady Luck is zooming through the zenith of your chart, 1995 can be the most profitable year you have experienced for some time. Whether you choose to come out on top very much depends on your own attitude and on no account should you use other people as an excuse to splash out. Naturally, no one can prevent you from spending modestly on the occasional good causes, and no one would wish to do so. Despite this, try to remember how easily you have been

taken in with a good sob story. If you are considering
distributing some of your largesse do make checks as
you could easily be fooled into giving to undeserved
charities.

Armed with this information, you are sure to enjoy
a prosperous and successful year – the rest, Pisces, is
entirely up to you. Refer to the monthly and daily guides
and take particular note of the position of Mars as this
will help you to make the most of the year ahead.

Love and Sex Year

When it comes to sex, you are clearly all male or all female, right down to your last pubic hair – providing you have any, that is, for the Piscean woman could well believe that pubic hair is ugly and dispose of it.

While no one would ever describe you as exactly masochistic, you do have a distinct inclination towards devoting yourself to your partner and allowing yourself to be dominated. This excites you and makes you feel fully aware of your sexuality.

Of course, you possess a vivid imagination, and your fantasies reflect your needs, if in an exaggerated form. More than any other sign, the Piscean woman fantasizes about rape. She may also dream of being forced into prostitution and, while the reality would certainly nauseate her, may enjoy hearing about such things in the heat of the moment, or she may be stimulated by pornography on this subject.

The male Piscean has similar fantasies and partner swopping could also enter his head. Although he is unlikely to admit to this, given the right circumstances it could occur. Subtle hints could be thrown out and it would take only a few drinks and a direct order for the fantasy to change into reality before his mate really knows what has happened.

If there were sexual ratings of some kind, the fish must be described as highly-sexed, pliable, but extremely romantic and sensitive. Anyone who really cares about you must think twice before involving you in any kind of deviation with a third party as this is sure to lead to unpleasant repercussions. For you, it is always wise to make it known to your partner that regardless of what you may or may not say within the bedroom, it is only an idea which seems valid at the time and one that is often used as a prop for added stimulation and titillation. Otherwise, certain signs could become confused and unsettled.

The most potent aphrodisiac for you is romance. You long to be swept away by a 'grand passion'. And with your Pisces imagination you are able to persuade yourself that this is occurring whenever the fancy takes you. Yes, Pisces, it is no small wonder that those who become involved with you tend to emerge somewhat puzzled. With members of this sign there is a thin line between fact and fantasy which has always been difficult to define.

As for 1995, are you more or less likely to settle down during this period? The answer to this question lies in the position of Jupiter and Saturn. On the one hand, you will be enjoying greater prosperity and this will lead many of you into thinking that you can now afford to set up house. This is also encouraged by the fact that Saturn in your sign suggests that, just for once, you will not shrink from added responsibility. Therefore, it is quite possible that you will seriously consider making a long-lasting commitment to someone during this period.

For some of you, a more responsible attitude could lead to an attraction to those who come in the form of a 'package deal'. In other words, an involvement with someone with children is a strong possibility. However, bear in mind that whilst the urge to play Mummy or Daddy may be strong, offspring can conveniently be made to evaporate when you feel this particular fantasy has outlived its usefulness. Because of this, think long and hard before taking on board such a set of circumstances.

With lucky Jupiter sailing through the zenith of your chart, if you are fancy-free you may very well be drawn to members of the opposite sex met during your professional life. This may be a good thing as it suggests there are common interests.

The most likely times for meeting that special someone are during April and the second half of September.

As a Piscean it is always wise to remember that what may seem like a good idea today is quite likely to change tomorrow. And this is why you are quite frequently high on the list of divorce-prone Sun signs. Should you wish to remain single the monthly guides can certainly help you to retain that independence of yours.

If you are already involved in a serious relationship or married, extra responsibility is likely to come in the delightful form of an addition to the family. Increased prosperity will also encourage peace and harmony between yourself and that special someone in your life. Naturally, as a fish, there may be times when you will be tempted by those tasty little morsels on the side, particularly if you are a male of the species. In which case, may I suggest that you check out the months or weeks when you are most likely to be led astray and go out of your way to avoid this. Under no circumstances can you justify extra-marital fun by blaming it on the position of the planets, although, as a Piscean, you could very well try to do so.

With a little bit of effort 1995 holds forth a great deal of promise. Providing you can control the more negative side to your character, you will gain a great deal in the way of happiness as well as wisdom throughout this period. Always remember that in order to find your complete self, it is necessary to locate the right person. But on no account should you ever seriously consider compromising yourself simply because you are feeling temporarily lonely. After all, if you became engaged or married every time you were depressed you would end up with a closet full of wedding rings.

This year, more than any other, the stars may be helping you to recognize your own wants and needs as well as your weaknesses. Because of this you are likely to emerge a wiser and more contented fish and 1995 will remain in your memory and be thought about nostalgically later on in life.

Health and Diet Year

SPIRITUAL WELLBEING

Many people, including myself, are rapidly beginning to recognize the fact that mental attitude can and does have a direct effect on physical wellbeing. Some would argue that 'spiritual health' also plays a large part in maintaining a healthy body as well as a healthy mind. This is not to suggest that we must strive for 'sainthood' but, nevertheless, we should be aware of being on the right path – our journey towards some objective.

It is necessary to be conscious of our beliefs and our goals otherwise it is quite likely that we may lose our way and then our physical wellbeing may be affected by a sense of futility which can undermine our health. You know the kind of attitude: 'Is it really worth putting myself out?' 'I try but it doesn't seem to get me anywhere'. Most of us can recognize these feelings at some stages in our life. Should such an attitude occur and be followed by several unfortunate setbacks, which we all must occasionally experience, then this can initially dent our confidence and even more serious problems may occur if we allow ourselves to be pulled under. Believing we are getting nowhere seems to take all the joy out of life and certainly undermines our health. Deep down within our soul, we hunger for chances for growth and, when this is denied, how can we expect to retain bodily health if we lack the life or will to go on? Positive thinking can go a long way to keeping us hale and hearty. Perfect health encompasses the wholeness of mind, body and spirit.

HEALTH AND DIET

Because you are such a loving and sensitive individual you can be destroyed by unkindness or criticism. There is a general inclination for you to become emotionally and mentally drained by other people; this is counter-balanced by your strong need for privacy, which you find restorative. Furthermore it is also your way of avoiding unpleasantness, as is the Piscean tendency to turn to drugs and alcohol in an effort to escape. Luckily, with your unique intuition many of you appear to understand this danger and will not touch either. And where this is the case you are very wise or you are particularly prone to alcohol poisoning – and to poisoning from fish and water contamination.

You are, of course, inventive and intelligent, but inclined to escape into a fantasy world and you can spend too much time on your own day-dreaming. However, it must be pointed out that your inner world is real to you and your life can be richer and fuller by following your intuition and using it in constructive ways.

You possess a unique sense of rythmn and will probably enjoy aerobic exercises or simply dancing for pleasure. Either will help to keep you in peak condition.

When comparing you with your opposite sign of Virgo, it is noted that in common with this sign you possess adaptability and a desire to serve other people. Because of this both signs are inclined to suffer from intestine and stomach problems when upset or worried.

You are also the type that tends to ignore problems, but when this is impossible you try to get round them or away from them as quickly as possible. This is mainly because you easily become fretful and fearful and naturally this can lead to nervous disorders of all descriptions.

Psychologically, for the most part you are optimistic and happy. However, you do tend to fall prey to apprehension – sometimes because you sense coming events, but often because you anticipate things which never happen, and this often leads to unnecessary or avoidable stress.

In an ideal world, as a Piscean you should live near water and in natural conditions.

The parts of the body ruled by your sign are the pituitary and pineal glands, the duodenum, the lymphatic system and feet. It is fairly common for those born under this sign to suffer from glandular disorders, conjunctivitis, mucus in the lungs and foot problems.

Should you possess a natural inclination to be overweight this is likely to be chiefly because of a tendency to retain water. Nervous stress and drug allergies are pitfalls which need to be strenuously avoided.

Pisceans are likely to respond positively to herbal treatments and reflexology. Furthermore, exercise such as swimming and dancing can help you to relax rather than medication, which can be a way of life for you. As a Piscean you will also, no doubt, be happy fishing and sailing.

When it comes to diet it is wise to include liver, a great source of iron which you so badly need. Cucumbers, melons and almonds prove to be more nutritional to members of this sign than perhaps any other. You will find bilberries helpful to counteract water retention, arrow root to calm the stomach, and chicory to eliminate mucus.

Psychologically, you tend to underrate yourself and

be overly-concerned with the wellbeing of other people.
You need to understand this and avoid a natural willingness to carry other people's burdens. Like your fellow
sign of Cancer, you fear criticism and this can upset
your equilibrium.

You should strongly protect the privacy which you
need so much in order to renew yourself and find inner
peace. Otherwise you are likely to remain at the mercy
of every cold wind that blows through your life and may
decide to escape into psychosomatic illness. You are
perhaps the most impressionable of all the zodiac signs,
and can become a hypochondriac when life appears to
be getting on top of you. It would be wise to remember
that no one needs to be ill just because their constitution
has an inclination to a certain illness. A consciousness
of this as well as following a healthy regime can keep
you in disgustingly good health.

It was said by the 'Ancients' that most of us are able
to transmit some form of healing. As man has evolved,
this talent has been lost due to neglect, for all talents
need to be regularly used if they are not to waste away.
But whether this is true or not you can be sure that
each sign has something to contribute to the wellbeing
of mankind. As a water sign, you are, of course, very
suggestible and should actively seek to avoid those
suffering from illness, whether it be major or minor,
particularly if they insist on regaling you with details
of their symptoms in glorious prose. You recognize this
trait in yourself, too, but you have probably learnt to
control it. You are generally able to help other people in a
sympathetic but bracing way and, for this reason, many
doctors and nurses are born under the sign of Pisces.

How are you likely to fare during 1995? With Saturn
sailing through your sign, you could possibly experience a mid-life crisis involving the breakdown and
eventual destruction of collagen. Vitamin C can help

to delay this process: although it does not guarantee a sickness-free life, medical research has shown that this vitamin is as necessary as life itself. It helps to form collagen which keeps the cells a proper size and shape, enabling them to go about their business maintaining bodily health.

Furthermore, this sign tends to rule the skin and burns as well as teeth and ears. These, therefore, need to be treated with a great deal of respect during the year ahead. Luckily Saturn encourages a more responsible attitude to life and this may prevent you from taking unnecessary risks which could lead to breakages. An inclination to colds and flu is also likely to be helped considerably by the intake of vitamin C.

Other areas to watch this year include an inclination to over-indulge when in the company of workmates or contacts and minor burns and cuts when Mars is in opposition to your sign, that is, during January, June, and November. Luckily, regular checking in the monthly guides can help you to offset such unnecessary inconveniences. Therefore Pisces, you are once more in the driving seat and it is entirely up to you whether you manage to maintain an A1 condition, but because you are born under the sign of the Worrier, the chances are you won't be prepared to take any risks with your physical wellbeing. It looks, then, as if you have precious little to worry about.

Numerology Year

In order to discover the number of any year you are interested in, your 'individual year number', first take your birth date, day and month, and add this to the year you are interested in, be it in the past or in the future. As an example, say you were born on 9 August and you are interested in 1995:

$$
\begin{array}{r}
9 \\
8 \\
1995 \\
\hline
2012 \\
\hline
\end{array}
$$

Then, write down $2 + 0 + 1 + 2$ and you will discover this equals 5. This means that the number of your year is 5.

You can experiment with this method by taking any year from your past and discovering with the help of the following guide whether or not numerology works out for you.

The guide is perennial and applicable to all Sun signs: you can look up years for your friends as well as for yourself. Use it to discover general trends ahead, the way you should be approaching a chosen period and how you can make the most of the future.

INDIVIDUAL YEAR NUMBER 1

GENERAL FEEL

A time for being more self-sufficient and one when you should be ready to grasp the nettle. All opportunities must be snapped up, after careful consideration. Also an excellent time for laying down the foundations for future success in all areas.

DEFINITION

Because this is the number 1 individual year, you will have the chance to start again in many areas of life. The emphasis will be upon the new; there will be fresh faces in your life, more opportunities and perhaps even new experiences. If you were born on either the 1st, 19th or 28th and were born under the sign of Aries or Leo then this will be an extremely important time. It is crucial during this cycle that you be prepared to go it alone, push back horizons and generally open up your mind. Time also for playing the leader or pioneer wherever necessary. If you have a hobby which you wish to turn into a business, or maybe you simply wish to introduce other people to your ideas and plans, then do so whilst experiencing this individual cycle. A great period too for laying down the plans for long-term future gains. Therefore, make sure you do your homework well and you will be reaping the rewards at a later date.

RELATIONSHIPS

This is an ideal period for forming new bonds, perhaps business relationships, new friends and new loves too. You will be attracted to those in high positions and with strong personalities. There may also be an emphasis on bonding with people a good deal younger than yourself. If you are already in a long-standing relationship, then it is time to clear away the dead wood between you which may have been causing misunderstandings and unhappiness. Whether in love or business, you will find those who are born under the sign of Aries, Leo or Aquarius far more common in your life, also those born on the following dates: 1st, 4th, 9th, 10th, 13th, 18th, 19th, 22nd and 28th. The most important months for this individual year when you are likely to meet up with those who have a strong influence on you are January, May, July and October.

CAREER

It is likely that you have been wanting to break free and to explore fresh horizons in your job or in your career and this is definitely a year for doing so. Because you are in a fighting mood, and because your decision-making qualities as well as your leadership qualities are foremost, it will be an easy matter for you to find assistance as well as to impress other people. Major professional changes are likely and you will also feel more independent within your existing job. Should you want times for making important career moves, then choose Mondays or Tuesdays. These are good days for pushing your luck and presenting your ideas well. Changes connected with your career are going to be more likely during April, May, July and September.

HEALTH

If you have forgotten the name of your doctor or dentist, then this is the year for going for check-ups. A time too when people of a certain age are likely to start wearing glasses. The emphasis seems to be on eyes. Start a good health regime. This will help you cope with any adverse events that almost assuredly lie ahead. The important months for your own health as well as for loved ones are March, May and August.

INDIVIDUAL YEAR NUMBER 2

GENERAL FEEL

You will find it far easier to relate to other people.

DEFINITION

What you will need during this cycle is diplomacy, cooperation and the ability to put yourself in someone else's shoes. Whatever you began last year will now begin to show signs of progress. However, don't expect miracles; changes are going to be slow rather than at the speed of light. Changes will be taking place all around you. It is possible too that you will be considering moving from one area to another, maybe even to another country. There is a lively feel about domesticity and in relationships with the opposite sex too. This is going to be a marvellous year for making things come true and asking for favours. However, on no account should you force yourself and your opinions on other people. A spoonful of honey is going to get you a good deal further than a spoonful of vinegar. If you are born under the sign of Cancer or Taurus, or if your birthday falls on the 2nd, 11th, 20th or 29th, then this year is going to be full of major events.

RELATIONSHIPS

You need to associate with other people far more than is usually the case – perhaps out of necessity. The emphasis is on love, friendship and professional partnerships. The opposite sex will be much more prepared to get involved in your life than is normally the case. This is a year your chances of becoming engaged or married are increased and there is likely to be expansion in your family in the form of a lovely addition and also in the families of your friends and those closest to you. The instinctive and caring side to your personality is going to be strong and very obvious. You will quickly discover that you will be extra touchy and sensitive to things that other people say. Further, you will find those born under the sign of Cancer, Taurus and Libra entering your life far more than is usually the case. This also applies to those who are born on the 2nd, 6th, 7th, 11th, 15th, 20th, 24th, 25th or 29th of the month.

Romantic and family events are likely to be emphasized during April, June and September.

CAREER

There is a strong theme of change here, but there is no point in having a panic attack about that because, after all, life is about change. However, in this particular individual year any transformation or upheaval is likely to be of an internal nature, such as at your place of work, rather than external. You may find your company is moving from one area to another, or perhaps there are changes between departments. Quite obviously then the most important thing for you to do in order to make your life easy is to be adaptable. There is a strong possibility too that you may be given added responsibility. Do not flinch, this will bring in extra reward.

If you are thinking of searching for employment this year, then try to arrange all meetings and negotiations on Monday and Friday. These are good days for asking for favours or rises too. The best months are March, April, June, August, and December. All these are important times for change.

HEALTH

This individual cycle emphasizes stomach problems. The important thing for you is to eat sensibly, rather than going on, for example, a crash diet – which could be detrimental. If you are female then you would be wise to have a check-up at least once during the year ahead just to be sure you can continue to enjoy good health. All should be discriminating when dining out. Check cutlery, and take care if food has only been partially cooked. Furthermore, emotional stress could get you down, but only if you allow it. Provided you set aside some periods of relaxation in each day when you can close your eyes and let everything drift away then you will have little to worry about. When it comes to diet, be sure that the emphasis is on nutrition, rather than fighting the flab. Perhaps it would be a good idea to become less weight conscious during this period and let your body find its natural ideal weight on its own. The months of February, April, July and November may show health changes in some way. Commonsense is your best guide during this year.

INDIVIDUAL YEAR NUMBER 3

GENERAL FEEL

You are going to be at your most creative and imaginative during this time. There is a theme of expansion and growth and you will want to polish up your self-image in order to make the 'big impression'.

DEFINITION

It is a good year for reaching out, for expansion. Social and artistic developments should be interesting as well as profitable and this will help to promote happiness. There will be a strong urge in you to improve yourself, either your image or your reputation or perhaps your mind. Your popularity soars through the ceiling and this delights you. Involving yourself with something creative brings increased success plus a good deal of satisfaction. However, it is imperative that you keep yourself in a positive mood. This will attract attention and appreciation of all of your talents. Projects which were begun two years ago are likely to be sprouting this year. If you are born under the sign of Pisces or Sagittarius, or your birthday falls on the 3rd, 12th, 21st or 30th, then this year is going to be particularly special and successful.

RELATIONSHIPS

There is a happy-go-lucky feel about all your relationships and you are in a flirty, fancy-free mood. Heaven help anyone trying to catch you during the next twelve months: they will need to get their skates on. Relationships are likely to be ethereal and fun rather than heavy going. It is possible too that you will find yourself with those who are younger than you, particularly those born under the signs of Pisces and Sagittarius, and those whose birth dates add up to 3, 6 or 9. Your individual cycle shows important months for relationships are March, May, August and December.

CAREER

As I discussed earlier, this individual number is one that suggests branching out and personal growth, so be ready to take on anything new. Not surprisingly, your career aspects look bright and shiny. You are definitely going to be more ambitious and must keep up that positive façade and attract opportunities. Avoid taking obligations too flippantly; it is important that you adopt a conscientious approach to all your responsibilities. You may take on a fresh course of learning or look for a new job, and the important days for doing so would be on Thursday and Friday: these are definitely your best days. This is particularly true in the months of February, March, May, July and November: expect expansion in your life and take a chance during these times.

HEALTH

Because you are likely to be out and about painting the town all the colours of the rainbow, it is likely that some of your health problems could come through over-indulgence or perhaps tiredness. However, if you have got to have some health problems, I suppose these are the best ones to experience, because they are under your control. There is also a possibility that you may get a little fraught over work, which may result in some emotional scenes. However, you are sensible enough to realize they should not be taken too seriously. If you are prone to skin allergies, then these too could be giving you problems during this particular year. The best advice you can follow is not to go to extremes that will affect your body or your mind. It is all very well to have fun, but after a while too much not only affects your health but also the degree of enjoyment you experience. Take extra care between January and March, and June and October, especially where these are winter months for you.

INDIVIDUAL YEAR NUMBER 4

GENERAL FEEL

It is back to basics this year. Do not build on shaky foundations. Get yourself organized and be prepared to work a little harder than you usually do and you will come through without any great difficulty.

DEFINITION

It is imperative this year that you have a grand plan. Do not simply rush off without considering the consequences and avoid dabbling of all descriptions. It is likely too that you will be gathering more responsibility

and on occasions this could lead you to feeling unap-
preciated, claustrophobic and perhaps over-burdened
in some ways. Although it is true to say that this cycle
in your individual life tends to bring about a certain
amount of limitation, whether this be on the personal
side to life, the psychological or the financial, you now
have the chance to get yourself together and to build
on more solid foundations. Security is definitely your
key word at this time. When it comes to any project,
or job or plan, it is important that you ask the right
questions. In other words, do your homework before
you go off half cock. That would be a disaster. If you
are an Aquarius, a Leo or a Gemini or you are born
on the 4th, 13th, 22nd, or the 31st of any month, this
individual year will be extremely important and long
remembered.

RELATIONSHIPS

You will find that it is the eccentric, the unusual,
the unconventional, the downright odd, that will be
drawn into your life during this particular cycle. It
is also strongly possible that people you have not
met for some time may be re-entering your circle
and an older person or somebody outside your own
social or perhaps religious background will be drawn
to you too. When it comes to the romantic side of
things, again you are drawn to that which is different
from usual. You may even form a relationship with
someone who comes from a totally different background, perhaps from a distance. Something unusual
about them stimulates and excites you. Gemini, Leo
and Aquarius are your likely favourites, as well as
anyone whose birth number adds up to 1, 4, 5, or
7. Certainly the most exciting months for romance
are going to be February, April, July and November.
Make sure then that you put yourself about during

this particular time, and be ready for literally anything.

CAREER

Once more we have the theme of the unusual and different in this area of life. You may be plodding along in the same old rut when suddenly lightning strikes and you find yourself besieged by offers from other people and in a panic, not quite sure what to do. There may be a period when nothing particular seems to be going on, when to your astonishment you are given some promotion or some exciting challenge to take on board. Literally anything can happen in this particular cycle of your life. The individual year 4 also inclines towards added responsibilities and it is important that you do not offload them on to other people or cringe in fear. They will eventually pay off and in the meantime you will be gaining in experience and paving the way for greater success in the future. When you want to arrange any kind of meeting, negotiation or perhaps ask for any kind of favour at work, then try to do so on a Monday or a Wednesday for the luckiest results. January, February, April, October and November are certainly the months when you must play the opportunist and be ready to say yes to anything that comes your way.

HEALTH

The biggest problems that you will have to face this year are caused by stress, so it is important that you attend to your diet and are as philosophical as possible as well as ready to adapt to changing conditions. You are likely to find that people you thought you knew well are acting out of character and this throws you off balance. Take care too when visiting the doctor. Remember that you are dealing with a human being and that doctors, like the rest of us, can make mistakes. Unless you are 100 per cent satisfied then go for a second opinion over anything important. Try to be sceptical about yourself too because you are going to be a good deal more moody than usual. The times that need special attention are February, May, September and November. If any of these months fall in the winter part of your year, then wrap up well and dose up on vitamin C.

INDIVIDUAL YEAR NUMBER 5

GENERAL FEEL

There will be many more opportunities for you to get out and about and travel is certainly going to be playing a large part in your year. Change too must be expected and even embraced – after all, it is part of life. You will have more free time and choices, so all in all things look promising.

DEFINITION

It is possible that you tried previously to get something off the launching pad but for one reason or another, it simply didn't happen. Luckily, you now get a chance to renew those old plans and put them into action. You are certainly going to feel that things are changing for the better in all areas. You are going to be more actively involved with the public and will enjoy a certain amount of attention and publicity. You may have failed in the past but this year mistakes will be easier to accept and learn from, and you are going to find yourself both physically and mentally more in tune with your environment and with those you care about than ever before. If you are a Gemini or a Virgo or are born on the 5th,

14th or 23rd then this is going to be a period of major importance for you and you must be ready to take advantage of this.

RELATIONSHIPS

Lucky you! Your sexual magnetism goes through the ceiling and you will be involved in many relationships during the year ahead. You have that extra charisma about you which will be drawing others to you and you can look forward to being choosy. There will be an inclination to be drawn to those who are considerably younger than yourself. It is likely too that you will find that those born under the signs of Taurus, Gemini, Virgo and Libra as well as those whose birth date adds up to 2, 5 or 6 will play an important part in your year. The months for attracting others in a big way are January, March, June, October and December.

CAREER

This is considered by all numerologists as being one of the best numbers for self-improvement in all areas, and particularly on the professional front. It will be relatively easy for you to sell your ideas and yourself as well as to push your skills and expertise under the noses of other people. They will certainly sit up and notice. Clearly, then, a time for you to view the world as though it were your oyster and to get out there and grab your slice of the action. You have increased confidence and should be able to get exactly what you want. Friday and Wednesday are perhaps the best days if looking for a job or going to negotiations or interviews, or in fact for generally pushing yourself into the limelight. Watch out for March, May, September, October or December. Something of great importance could pop up at this time. There will certainly be a chance for advancement; whether you take it up or not is of course entirely up to you.

HEALTH

Getting a good night's rest could be your problem during the year ahead, since that mind of yours is positively buzzing and won't let you rest. Try turning your brain off at bedtime, otherwise you will finish up irritable and exhausted. Try to take things a step at a time without rushing around. Meditation may help you to relax and do more for your physical wellbeing than anything else. Because this is an extremely active year, you will need to do some careful planning so that you can cope with ease rather than rushing around like a demented mayfly. Furthermore, try to avoid going over the top with alcohol, food, sex, gambling or anything which could be described as 'get rich quick'. During January, April, August, and October, watch yourself a bit, you could do with some coddling, particularly if these happen to be winter months for you.

INDIVIDUAL YEAR NUMBER 6

GENERAL FEEL

There is likely to be increased responsibility and activity within your domestic life. There will be many occasions when you will be helping loved ones and your sense of duty is going to be strong.

DEFINITION

Activities for the most part are likely to be centred around property, family, loved ones, romance and your home. Your artistic appreciation will be good and you will be drawn to anything that is colourful and beautiful, and possessions that have a strong appeal to your eye or even your ear. Where domesticity is concerned, there is a strong suggestion that you may move out of one home into another. This is an excellent time too for self-education, for branching out, for graduating, for taking on some extra courses – whether simply to improve your appearance or to improve your mind. When it comes to your social life you are inundated with chances to attend social functions, such as openings of art galleries and facilities. You are going to be the real social butterfly flitting from scene to scene and enjoying yourself thoroughly. Try to accept nine out of ten invitations that come your way because they bring with them chances of advancement. If you are born on the 6th, 15th or 24th or should your birth sign be Taurus, Libra or Cancer then this is going to be a year that will be long remembered as a very positive one.

RELATIONSHIPS

When it comes to love, sex and romance the individual year 6 is perhaps the most successful. It is a time for being swept off your feet, for becoming engaged or for getting married. On the more negative side, perhaps there is separation and divorce. However the latter can be avoided, provided you are prepared to sit down and communicate properly. There is an emphasis too on pregnancy and birth, or changes in existing relationships. Circumstances will be sweeping you along. If you are born under the sign of Taurus, Cancer or Libra, then it is even more likely that this will be a major year for you, as well as for those born on dates adding up to 6, 3 or 2. The most memorable months of your year are going to be February, May,

September and November. Grab all opportunities to enjoy yourself and improve your relationships during these periods.

CAREER

A good year for this side to life too, with the chances of promotion and recognition for past efforts all coming your way. You will be able to improve your position in life even though lately it is likely you have been frustrated. On the cash front big rewards will come flooding in mainly because you are prepared to fulfil your obligations and commitments without complaint or protest. Other people will appreciate all the efforts you have put in, so plod along and you will find your efforts will not be in vain. Perversely, if you are looking for a job or setting up an interview, negotiation or a meeting, or simply want to advertise your talents in some way, then your best days for doing so are Monday, Thursday and Friday. Long-term opportunities are very strong during the months of February, April, August, September and November. These are the key periods for pushing yourself up the ladder of success.

HEALTH

If you are to experience any problems of a physical nature during this year, then they could be tied up with the throat, nose or the tonsils plus the upper parts of the body. Basically what you need to stay healthy during this year is plenty of sunlight, moderate exercise, fresh air and changes of scene. Escape to the coast too if this is at all possible. The months for being particularly watchful are March, July, September and December. Think twice before doing anything during this time and there is no reason why you shouldn't stay hale and hearty for the whole year.

INDIVIDUAL YEAR NUMBER 7

GENERAL FEEL

A year for inner growth and for finding out what really makes you tick and what you need to make you happy. Self-awareness and discovery are all emphasized during the individual year 7.

DEFINITION

You will be provided with the opportunity to place as much emphasis as possible on your personal life and your own wellbeing. There will be many occasions when you will find yourself analysing your past motives and actions, and developing a need to give more attention to your own personal needs, goals and desires. There will also be many occasions when you will feel the need to escape any kind of confusion, muddle or noise, and time spent alone will not be wasted. It will give you time for meditation and also for examining exactly where you have come to so far and where you want to go in the future. It is important you make up your mind what you want out of this particular year because once you have done this you will attain those ambitions. Failure to do so could mean you end up chasing your tail and that is a pure waste of time and energy. You will also discover that secrets about yourself and other people could be surfacing during this year. If you are born under the sign of Pisces or Cancer, or on the 7th, 16th or 25th of the month, then this year will be especially wonderful.

RELATIONSHIPS

It has to be said from the word go that this is not the best year for romantic interest. A strong need for contemplation will mean spending time on your own. Any romance that does develop this year may not live up to your great expectations, but, providing you are prepared to take things as they come without jumping to conclusions, then you will enjoy yourself without getting hurt. Decide exactly what it is you have in mind and then go for it. Romantic interests this year are likely to be with people who are born on dates that add up to 2, 4 or 7 or with people born under the sign of Cancer or Pisces. Watch for romantic opportunities during January, April, August and October.

CAREER

When we pass through this particular individual cycle, two things in life tend to occur: retirement from the limelight, or a general slowing down, perhaps by taking leave of absence or maybe retraining in some way. It is likely too that you will become more aware of your own occupational expertise and skills – you will begin to understand your true purpose in life and will feel much more enlightened. Long-sought-after goals begin to come to life if you have been drifting of late. The best attitude to have throughout the year is an exploratory one when it comes to your work. If you want to set up negotiations, interviews or meetings, arrange them for Monday or Friday. In fact any favours you seek should be tackled on these days. January, March, July, August, October and December are particularly good for self-advancement.

HEALTH

Since, in comparison to previous years, this is a rather quiet time, health problems are likely to be minor. Some will possibly come through irritation or worry and the best thing to do is to attempt to remain meditative and calm. This state of mind will bring positive results. Failure to do so may create unnecessary problems by allowing your imagination to run completely out of control. You need time this year to restore, recuperate and contemplate. Any health changes that do occur are likely to happen in February, June, August and November.

INDIVIDUAL YEAR NUMBER 8

GENERAL FEEL

This is going to be a time for success, for making important moves and changes, a time when you may gain power and certainly one when your talents are going to be recognized.

DEFINITION

This individual year gives you the chance to 'think big', a time you can occupy the limelight and wield power. If you were born on the 8th, 17th or 26th of the month or come under the sign of Capricorn, pay attention to this year and make sure you make the most of it. You should develop greater maturity and will discover a true feeling of faith and destiny, both in yourself and in events that occur. This is a cycle connected with career, ambition and money, but debts from the past will have to be re-paid. For example, an old responsibility or debt that you may have avoided in past years may reappear to haunt you. However, whatever you do with this twelve months, aim high – think big, think success and above all be positive.

RELATIONSHIPS

This particular individual year is one which is strongly connected with birth, divorce and marriage – most of the landmarks we experience in life in fact. Lovewise, those who are more experienced or older than you, or someone of power, authority, influence or wealth will be very attractive. This year will be putting you back in touch with those from your past – old friends, comrades, associates, and even romances from long ago crop up once more. You should not experience any great problems romantically this year, especially if you are dealing with Capricorns or Librans, or with those whose date of birth adds up to 8, 6 or 3. The best months for romance to develop are likely to be March, July, September and December.

CAREER

The number 8 year is generally believed to be the best one when it comes to bringing in cash. It is also good for asking for a rise or achieving promotion or authority over other people. This is your year for bathing in the limelight of success, the result perhaps of your past efforts. Now you will be rewarded. Financial success is all but guaranteed, provided you keep faith with your ambitions and yourself. It is important that you set major aspirations for yourself and work slowly towards them. You will be surprised how easily they are fulfilled. Conversely, if you are looking for work, then do set up interviews, negotiations and meetings, preferably on Saturday, Thursday or Friday, which are your luckiest days. Also watch out for chances to do yourself a bit of good during February, June, July, September and November.

HEALTH

You can avoid most health problems, particularly headaches, constipation or liver problems, by avoiding moods of depression, and feelings of loneliness. It is important when these descend that you keep yourself busy enough not to dwell on them. When it comes to receiving attention from the medical profession you would be well advised to get a second opinion. Eat wisely, try to keep a positive and enthusiastic outlook on life and all will be well. Periods which need special care are January, May, July and October. Therefore, if these months fall during the winter part of your year, wrap up and dose yourself with vitamins.

INDIVIDUAL YEAR NUMBER 9

GENERAL FEEL

A time for tying up the loose ends. Wishes are likely to be fulfilled and matters brought to swift conclusions. Inspirations run amok. Much travel is likely.

DEFINITION

The number 9 individual year is perhaps the most successful of all. It tends to represent the completion of matters and affairs, whether in work, business, or personal affairs. Your ability to let go of habits, people and negative circumstances or situations, that may have been holding you back, is strong. The sympathetic and humane side to your character also surfaces and you learn to give more freely of yourself without expecting anything in return. Any good deeds that you do will certainly be well rewarded, in terms of satisfaction and perhaps financially too. If you are born under the sign of Aries or Scorpio, or on the 9th, 18th or 27th of the month, this is certainly going to be an all important year.

RELATIONSHIPS

The individual year 9 is a cycle which gives appeal as well as influence. Because of this, you will be getting emotionally tied up with members of the opposite sex who may be outside your usual cultural or ethnic group. The reason for this is that this particular number relates to humanity and of course this tends to quash ignorance, pride and bigotry. You also discover that Aries, Leo and Scorpio people are going to be much more evident in your domestic affairs, as well as those whose birth dates add up to 9, 3 or 1. The important months for relationships are February, June, August and November. These will be extremely hectic and eventful from a romantic viewpoint and there are times when you could be swept off your feet.

CAREER

This is a year which will help to make many of your dreams and ambitions come true. Furthermore it is an excellent time for success if you are involved in marketing your skills, your talents and your expertise on a broader level. You may be thinking of expanding abroad for example and if so this is certainly a good idea. You will find that harmony and cooperation with your co-workers or those who work for you are easier than before and this will help your dreams and ambitions. The best days for you if you want to line up meetings or negotiations are going to be Tuesday and Thursday and this also applies if you are looking for employment or want a special day for doing something of an ambitious nature. Employment or business changes could also feature during January, May, June, August and October.

HEALTH

The only physical problem you may have during this particular year is accidents, so be careful. Try too to avoid unnecessary tension and arguments with other people. Take extra care when you are on the roads:

no drinking and driving for example. You will only have problems if you play your own worst enemy. Be extra watchful when in the kitchen or bathroom: sharp instruments that you find in these areas can lead to cuts being commonplace, unless you take care.

Monthly Guide

JANUARY

Before writing in any particular depth about this month, it might be an idea to remind you of the lesson you are supposed to be learning up until August. The stars suggest that you have been able to establish yourself and can now relate to your immediate environment better, including neighbours and relatives. You have also been able to benefit in this area of life through education, travel and improved lines of communication. A little discipline has been learnt and it is time now to turn your attention elsewhere. You must learn how to use the resources acquired by contact with other people in your wider relationships. Work, too, on increasing your perceptions and, above all, listen to them: they are likely to bring knowledge, inspiration and wider vision. Further education and prolonged travelling will serve to both broaden and develop your mind. Therefore, during the ensuing months grab any opportunity to take this lesson on board and enrich your life.

During January, Pluto will temporarily enter Sagittarius on the 19th, although it is only likely to affect those born during the last two days of the Piscean period. Should this apply to you, you may find your progress prone to sudden fits and starts. Nevertheless, if you persist in all your efforts, Jupiter will help you to reap rewards later in the year.

Venus will enter the zenith of your chart on the 8th of the month, making this a particularly lucky period for professional partnerships, creativity of all descriptions, and the arts. Regardless of your profession, life will seem easier and more hopeful in the working environment. You are likely to be socializing with professional contacts more than usual and many of you may even be attracted to a colleague. If you are already in a steady relationship, it will take all your will-power to resist the temptation to give in to mild flirtations. Quite frankly, it is certainly not worth entertaining the thought if it means jeopardizing a close bond you may have forged with someone else. Certainly, when chances to have fun occur, you would be well advised to take your mate along – just in case you are tempted.

The Sun occupies the sign of Capricorn up until the 20th, increasing the confidence of all Pisceans who are employed in administration, team work or in any job where it is necessary to take the initiative and drum up business.

The influence of friends seems to be good and positive during January and they will be persuading you to join them socially far more than usual. Your visits to clubs, both sporting and otherwise, are likely to be above average for this time of the year. Furthermore, during the first week Mercury's placing in Capricorn suggests new contacts will rapidly become friends, and these people could be a good deal younger than yourself.

From the 7th onwards, Mercury moves into the sign of Aquarius. This will tend to increase your intuition and perceptions and make you more contemplative. You may also discover at a later date that those closest to you have been keeping secrets, perhaps out of necessity. Generally, work which is carried out in the background – for example research – will be thriving and helping you in some way in the near future.

Romantically, during the first week of the month you may be drawn to those who are involved in higher education, long-distance travel, or legal matters. However, there is an instability in such relationships so you should not take them too seriously. Avoid the temptation to become completely carried away in one of your Piscean fantasies.

Financially, during the first three weeks, you will be easily led into impulse buying, which you are sure to regret at a later date. But forewarned is forearmed and you do not necessarily have to fall into this trap. Naturally, as a fish you have no great desire to accumulate a tremendous amount of wealth, but even you must admit that a roof over your head and food in your stomach are prerequisites for a peaceful existence.

Healthwise, it is an ideal time of the year to visit the dentist, particularly if you have forgotten his name. This will help to offset the tendency of Saturn in Pisces to encourage cavities in those molars of yours. As a Piscean, you have a natural inclination to procrastinate in this area. However, should you do so, you will be stirring up a good deal of trouble for yourself in the near future. Why invite trouble when a quick check-up can put your mind at ease and help to maintain healthy teeth.

Sexually, the placing of Mars in your opposition up until the 23rd will certainly be sending the adrenaline pounding through your veins, and whilst there is no reason why you should not satisfy your natural urges, it would be a good idea to take the necessary precautions, particularly in this day and age. In doing so you can feel free to give free rein to those lusty urges, especially if you are single.

January is rarely a hectic month for you but this year will be providing you with ample opportunity to meet new faces – and 'people contact' always helps to keep you in high spirits. For you this happens to be half the battle when tackling other sides to life. Therefore, be ready to socialize in the company of those who amuse you and help you to relax.

Luckily, this month you are blessed with two new Moons, and the first occurs in the sign of Capricorn on the 1st. This seems to suggest that you will be meeting many new people and quickly establishing close contact with those who can be both useful and a boon to your life. New Moons provide us with an opportunity to make fresh starts so if you have been laying down a master plan for the rest of your life this is as good a time as any for leaping into action.

The full Moon falls in the sign of Cancer on the 16th. Try to be your usual fluid and adaptable self as last-minute changes may occur to social arrangements. However, don't allow this to bring you down as these changes are likely to be a vast improvement on your existing plans. Should you need to work out what needs to be done, in order to get a romance back on the tracks, this is the ideal time for making plans, although not necessarily for leaping into action. Finishing touches to artistic work will be adding just the right touch and will make all the difference.

The second new Moon this month occurs in the sign of Aquarius on the 30th. You are strongly advised at this time to listen to your intuitions. Further, your imagination is running riot and needs controlling in order to benefit you in some way. Those of you who work in the background are likely to receive some exciting news.

FEBRUARY

For the majority of this month, and well up to the 19th anyway, the Sun will be squatting in the sign of Aquarius – off and on throughout this period there will be times when you will opt for quiet and seclusion, but you must ensure that this does not lead to brooding or encourage that imagination to cloud your perspective. You will most certainly be aware of life's undercurrents and this will help you to instinctively know what action needs to be taken in any given area at any given time. Should you work in the medical profession, whilst life may be as hectic as usual, it will also be more rewarding.

Financially, you could suddenly develop a longing for luxurious objects after the 24th. However, unless you can afford to splash out in such an irresponsible fashion, it is suggested that you try to keep a tight control on your bank account at this time.

Mars' move into Leo suggests that you are likely to become physically attracted to those in positions of power and influence, or perhaps to people far more successful than yourself. It is important to understand that you are not truly attracted to what is inside, merely to the trimmings of success; once you accept this fact you can enjoy yourself without confusing your physical with your emotional needs.

Romantically, Venus moves into the sign of Capricorn on the 5th, suggesting that if you happen to be fancy-free you may meet someone special, either through an introduction made by a friend or perhaps whilst visiting a club. Certainly, Venus in this position will be throwing a harmonious glow over your friendship circle and if you need any kind of favour you should not hesitate to ask as others are at their most obliging and generous.

Mercury will be moving into direct movement again on the 17th, so delay dealing with legal matters, important paperwork and contracts until after this date. Otherwise you could be making life unnecessarily complicated for yourself and it is so easily avoidable.

Furthermore, be as self-sufficient as you can during the first three weeks of this month because although outwardly other people may seem eager to please and be informative, it is quite likely that they are deficient in some way and may have misinterpreted facts which they are passing on to you.

Should you be in a steady relationship you may find your mate somewhat preoccupied. It seems as though they are wrestling with problems and for reasons best known to themselves are either unwilling or unable to confide in you for the time being. Avoid thinking the worst. When the time is right they will come out into the open with their intentions, confident that their research or soul-seeking has produced correct and positive results.

Perhaps the best period of the month is from the 19th onwards when the Sun will be entering your sign. It is a time when your confidence and belief in yourself will be on the increase. Your sunny disposition will attract not only the opposite sex but also opportunities, and you must be quick to snap them up as rarely do you receive a second chance to take a bite out of such a particularly luscious cherry.

Healthwise, apart from an inclination to dwell a little bit too much on the past, you should be in A1 condition. However, in order to prevent that imagination of yours from running away with you, be sure that you keep yourself mentally occupied at all times. Remember, too, that your intuitions are spot on throughout this month and you should back them to the hilt, particularly when it comes to judging character or deciding on the correct time for particular action.

Now for a look at the state of the Moon.

Last month we were spoilt with two new Moons and we are therefore completely deserted by this particular planetary phenomenon during February. However, there is a full Moon on the 15th in the sign of Leo, making an excellent period for laying down plans for the future. It is also a time when you may swiftly reach the conclusion that a relationship has long outlived its usefulness, despite the fact that you have fought hard and long to keep it going. Perhaps it would be wise to allow the full Moon to pass before making that final decision, but once this has occurred, if you are still of the same opinion, my advice to you is to sweep this negative influence out of your life once and for all.

February, then, seems to be a time for affection and deep thought. Luckily, next month will provide you with a chance to act in a big way.

MARCH

March is, of course, your time of the year – a period when you are at your most independent, responsible, authoritative and strong-willed. Generally speaking, you are playing a prominent role in all events that are going on around you. Mercury, too, will be entering your sign on the 15th, arousing your curiosity, encouraging a shrewd attitude to finance, and making you more physically active and excitable. As a fish you are very seldom short of words and during this month you are at your most eloquent. Because of this, if you are involved with sales or anything where persuasive powers are needed on a professional level, you will certainly be doing well for yourself.

On a more personal level, Mercury will be encouraging your sense of humour, although there could be a tendency to jump to conclusions and this should be discouraged.

The last two weeks of the month are an ideal time for making minor changes in life or adjustments to existing plans. Many new people are likely to enter your life and this all helps to make for an extremely lively period. Should you be completely unattached, from the 15th onwards the need to be with people will be very real and strong and you will need to plan as full a social life as possible. Not that this should be difficult: you are at your most popular and people seem to be clamouring for your company.

On a professional level, this is an excellent month for those of you who are freelance workers or self-employed. It is lucky, too, should you need to make any professional changes or attempt to get backing for your ideas. Others will be only too willing and able to extend a helping hand. However, if your work requires a great deal of concentration, after the 15th you may need to double-check everything as your mind is racing along at the speed of light and minor mistakes are a possibility, although with a little bit of common sense this is a pitfall which can easily be avoided.

Socially, you are ready to take on board new intellectual pursuits, meet new people and travel further for the sake of having fun. Certainly you are going to be a boon to any environment and your popularity seems to be at an all-time high.

Romantically, the month slightly favours those already in relationships, although if you are fancy-free a friend may be making interesting introductions between the 3rd and the 23rd, and because of this you should not decline any invitations that come your way. Friendship is, of course, always an important part of your life and you will discover this month that others are only too happy to ply you with any kind of help or assistance that is needed.

The Sun enters Aries on the 21st making this a good time for chasing money which is owed or trying to generate more of that nasty stuff which causes us so many difficulties.

Healthwise, there may be a slight inclination to exhaustion after the 15th, but this is only an indication that your life is jam-packed with socializing and that you must not neglect to set aside one or two nights to recouperate. Should you observe this advice you will remain your normal robust self.

Your cash planet Mars will resume direct movement on the 24th and from our position in space appears to be in backward movement. However, after this date any complications which you may have been plagued with recently slowly begin to evaporate and you can push ahead, especially where monies are owed, with confidence and good humour.

Finally, should an opportunity arise for you to take on extra responsibility, instead of swimming in the opposite direction as you normally would, it might be a good idea to stop and consider. Although you tend to shy away from added burdens, in this particular instance they could lead to greater reward. Listen to the advice of older and more experienced people, particularly where long-standing problems are concerned, because it is likely that they can pass on useful tips which will help you to extract the maximum from your month.

This is an important month for you, Pisces, and a time when you must make an all-out effort to realize your hopes, wishes and dreams. Otherwise you could regret it at a later date and this is so unnecessary.

Because we were devoid of a new Moon last month, we are now given two as in January. The first occurs on the 1st of the month in your own sign. This is a time when your feelings will be prominent and you will be at your most romantic, imaginative and sensitive to your environment. Should the chance to travel arise, or should you need to make changes, do not hesitate to do so. As always, new Moons provide us with an opportunity to make fresh starts. This is particularly true on this day. Furthermore, you will be enjoying a great deal of attention and must use this period well for extracting favours or chasing work.

The full Moon during March occurs on the 17th in your opposite sign of Virgo. Because of this it is likely that in one of your relationships, feelings that may have been bubbling beneath the surface now begin to rise. In a way you will feel relieved because at least you now know where you stand with someone who is important to you. Should you have been considering jettisoning someone from your life, this is an ideal time for doing so. It is also a propitious period for making plans for the future.

The second new Moon this month falls in the sign of Aries, the cash area of life. Money can be gained from the female race, public commodities and even liquids. You are also especially sensitive to public needs at this time and if you require these talents on a professional level you will certainly be doing well. There is a strong chance, too, that you may be treated to a fresh source of income. So get out into life and be ready to say 'yes' to Lady Luck when she strays across your path. Some of you may acquire a new possession, perhaps in the form of a late birthday present, although it could equally be a bonus of some description.

Remember that March is an important month and it is up to you to maximize your good fortune.

APRIL

Up until the 21st the Sun will be squatting in the sign of Aries, the cash area of your life. It must be remembered that without this planet there would be no life: it is the driving force behind the whole solar system. it represents will-power, vitality, leadership, creativity, and the urge to achieve your conscious aims, and these qualities should be channelled into financial matters during the month ahead. Furthermore, you can gain through government bodies and influential people and are also likely to be generous, magnanimous and strongly drawn to status symbols.

If you are professionally involved or in banking or finance you can expect a productive time. For other members of this sign, it is an ideal time for attempting to acquire backing for your ideas and calling in monies which are owed. In addition, Mercury occupies Aries between the 2nd and the 17th, bringing financial gains through travel, advertising, publishing, agencies and journalism. Certainly your financial skill is improving and you will be valuing things by their immediate usefulness to you. Those of you who collect books are likely to be adding to this collection.

Romantically, you are likely to be more emotionally sensitive than usual – sensation-seeking even. However, you will also be more charitable and unselfish, characteristics which will draw the opposite sex to you. Unfortunately, up until the 22nd there is a need for caution where romance is concerned as other people may not be quite as honest and forthright as you are at this time. A little bit of digging around in the background could save you a considerable amount of hurt. But once Venus enters your sign on the 22nd you will be at your most affectionate, pleasant, cheerful, sociable, sympathetic, artistic and hard to resist. Those who enter your life late in the month are likely to mean a great deal to you for some time to come, and this is an ideal period for engagements and marriages.

Because Mercury occupies the sign of Aries between the 2nd and the 16th, it is likely that you can gain through interviews, paperwork, legal affairs and taking the initiative. You are likely to be far more shrewd than usual and other people will need to be up early if they are to take advantage of you, which is extremely unlikely. Furthermore, you will find that influential people will be only too happy to help you in any way they can and you must not hesitate to ask for help should it be required.

For the majority of the month Venus will be occupying your sign. Because of this you will be physically and mentally irresistible: affectionate, pleasant, cheerful and sociable. You really couldn't have a better time for forming relationships with new people who enter your life, and they are likely to be around for some considerable time. A good time, too, for engagements and marriages.

Many born under the sign of Pisces possess creative talent. Sometimes this is used as a recreational hobby but often the fish is drawn to a creative job. If this applies to you, you will certainly be making a big impression.

In general this is not a month for playing the shrinking violet. Instead draw attention to your talents and skills – and expect a certain amount of appreciation.

Because Jupiter moves into retrograde action on the 2nd – and from our position in space appears to be going backwards – you may need to be a little more patient when it comes to realizing your professional hopes and wishes. However, providing you are able to do this, you can be confident of success in the near future.

Healthwise, there is clearly a tendency to over-indulge up until the 22nd, but as long as you avoid the temptation to drink and drive, you may decide that the ensuing hangover or stomach upset was well worth while. Hopefully, though, you will not make any emotional or sexual commitments whilst under the influence, which would be typical of your sign.

April certainly promises to be a productive, happy

and rewarding month. It is a time to be adventurous
and optimistic for in this way you will draw all the good
things to you. Should you for one moment believe you
are about to sink into one of your famous moods of
insecurity, seek out the company of those who are able
to boost your spirits. By helping yourself in this way
you can make April one of the most important months
of the year.

The full Moon this month occurs on the 15th in the
sign of Libra and as usual this is an excellent time for
laying down plans for the future. It is also a time for
discarding old habits, negative responses and pulling
out of situations which are no longer productive, and
that includes relationships.

MAY

The Sun this month will certainly have a positive effect
on your state of mind as well as your outlook on life,
helping to make you impartial instead of constantly
ruled by your emotions. It will encourage your creativity and self-reliance – making this a cheerful, lively
and constructive period. You will want to keep on
the go as much as possible and will be taking trips
for the slightest reason. Relationships with relatives
and neighbours enjoy a positive phase, too. Students
will find their concentration increased and studies will
sink in faster. Other Pisceans will develop a temporary
need to spread knowledge and apply past experience to
situations, which can only benefit other people.

Venus will be entering Taurus on the 18th, enhancing
your artistic appreciation and giving you a bright, hopeful approach to life. You will experience the need to visit
harmonious, peaceful and beautiful surroundings and
will reject anything that is crude or tasteless.

There is certainly a rosy glow over professional matters if you are involved in buying, selling, transport or any other mental pursuit.

Financially, the first eighteen days of the month are time for positive action, especially if you are trying to sell your creative ideas to other people. Monies which are owed can easily be retrieved, providing you are prepared to turn on the charm. Many of you will be deriving every opportunity to swell your bank account, and once you have taken professional advice you can push ahead in an effort to improve the materialistic side of life.

Mercury will be squatting in the sign of Gemini from the 3rd onwards, which will aid those of you with any literary talents. It will also be a great time for studying and it is likely that many of you will be taking work home in order to catch up. Regardless of your age, young people will be influencing your life more than usual. And home entertaining, perhaps with new people, seems to be the norm rather than the exception.

You may also be considering a change of residence. If so, you should leap into action as it should not be difficult to find your ideal abode at a reasonable price. Unfortunately, Mercury goes into backward movement from the 24th onwards; if you need to travel, sign documents or chase work, try to do so before this date as muddle and confusion could result from this particular placing.

Mars will be moving into your opposite sign of Virgo on the 26th. This is likely to have a twofold effect: firstly, the adrenaline certainly seems to be pounding through your veins and you will be on the look out for instant and immediate sexual gratification. Certainly there is no reason why you should not enjoy yourself, but do take care. Secondly, if you are in a steady relationship you may expect your partner to be far more energetic and lustful than usual. One way or the other, it looks as if you are in for an interesting month. However, it is important not to confuse sex with love: an easy pitfall at this moment in time.

Financially, you will discover that other people are only too willing to lend a helping hand, whether it be for advice or constructive criticism. Financial gains can be made in professional partnerships or whilst working in harness with others.

Healthwise, the opposition from the planet Mars could be making you more impulsive than usual and you need to slow down when moving around from one area to another. Look out for objects lying on the floor, and take particular care when in the kitchen or bathroom. It is unlikely that anything untoward will occur but preventative action is always preferable if there is even the remotest chance of mishaps.

The Sun's placing in Taurus for the majority of the month makes the first two weeks an ideal time for brushing aside past misunderstandings with relatives or neighbours. Ensure that you are the first one to make a move as this will be well received and you can resolve to start again.

May looks as if it is going to be a productive but energetic time. It is likely that you will have reason to have high hopes, and with a little bit of practical application there is no reason why you should not be able to turn those dreams into reality.

This month the full Moon occurs in the sign of Scorpio on the 14th. Try to avoid making any ambitious moves at this time as it is unlikely that you will be in possession of all the facts, which may only come to light once you have made a false start. Certainly make plans, but choose your moment carefully before you implement them.

The new Moon occurs in the sign of Gemini on the

29th. At this time your yearning for inner peace and security will be increased and there may be a chance for you to fulfil this desire in a practical fashion. On the home front there is likely to be increased activity and some of you may actually gain public recognition. Should you be a younger reader, it is likely that your mother's influence will be extra strong during this period. Her actions and advice are well meaning and it may be a good idea to digest what you have been told as you may be able to benefit in some way in the future. Those of you who are entertaining at home during this period, or perhaps looking for somewhere new to live, should be lucky at this time. As ever, new Moons are a time for fresh starts: do not hesitate to leap into action wherever you deem it necessary.

JUNE

For the majority of this month, up until the 22nd at least, the Sun will be squatting in the sign of Gemini, encouraging stability, pride in your domestic environment, and enhancing the good and positive influences that your parents may have exercised on you.

Professionally speaking, this is an ideal time for those involved with property and its allied trades – and for the homeworker and those who want to beautify their surroundings.

Luckily, Mercury resumes forward movement from the 17th onwards; therefore, leave to one side anything connected with paperwork, documents, legal matters, travel or job interviews until after this date. Should it be necessary to move before then, refer to the daily guides for a lucky day. Mercury's placing in Gemini suggests that younger people may be influencing your life in a good and positive way; it will certainly be helpful if you are at all studious or involved in the literary world. All Pisceans will be making more contacts with a wide range of people, even though these may be basically superficial. Nevertheless, it will make for a lively and stimulating period.

Should you work in an artistic or creative field, use the first eleven days of this month to draw attention to your talents. After this time, Venus will be moving into Gemini and increasing in you a desire to entertain – and, I might add, in some style. This is due to the fact that you will be taking a certain amount of pride in your home and many of you will want to make it more attractive. All Pisceans will certainly be sensitive to their environment and atmospheres between people. Because of this it might be a good idea to spend your time with those who seem to be at peace with one another rather than warring factions which will only disturb your equilibrium.

Romantically, this is hardly the most important month of your life. Nevertheless, you seem to be in a flirty mood and more than willing to settle for brief encounters rather than searching for a special 'soul mate'. Consequently, June probably favours those of you already in relationships, where a cosy atmosphere seems to prevail.

Regardless of your marital status, the placing of Mars in your opposite sign of Virgo continues to encourage your physical needs, especially those of a sexual nature. Despite this, just for once you are not confusing love with sex and are quite happy to fulfil your needs whenever the opportunity arises.

On the work front you will discover that colleagues are in an energetic, imaginative but pushy frame of mind. It may pay you to go along with their ideas.

In order to retain your usual good health it will be necessary to ensure periods of true relaxation when you can close your eyes and allow the world to drift away. Better still, why not enrol in a course of yoga, or some other form of relaxation such as meditation. Pisces frequently benefit from these methods of maintaining good health.

Few true Pisceans are sporty. However, there are bound to be exceptions to the rule due to other influences in the birthchart. If this applies to you, take a little extra care as impulsiveness could lead to minor mishaps. In order to avoid such a state of affairs refer to the daily tables.

This month the full Moon occurs on the 13th in the sign of Sagittarius at the zenith of your chart, making this an ideal time for putting the finishing touches to work before launching into anything new. Furthermore, there may also be a certain amount of scandal going the rounds, but if you are wise you will side-step any personal involvement. Should you deal with the public, you may find it extremely difficult to hold on to your temper during this period, but ideally you should strive to do so. As always, this is an excellent time for making plans, especially where professional matters are concerned.

The new Moon during June occurs in the sign of Cancer on the 28th, suggesting that you will be enjoying a couple of days when you will be on the constant search for pleasure and romance, and you should not be disappointed. However, you are at your most flirty and should be discouraged from making commitments for the time being. There may also be opportunities to attend an exciting social occasion – certainly your pleasure-seeking impulses are strong at this moment in time. As ever, new Moons are just the time for making fresh starts and meeting new people. Sporting endeavours are likely to be lucky for you during this period, although a tendency to speculate should be avoided – unless, of course, you are involving yourself in such a way that you are using money which you can well afford to lose.

June seems to have a lively feel about it, even though one aspect of life may be giving you a certain amount of worry. Continue to think positively, act constructively and this will soon cease to be a problem.

JULY

For you, July tends to be a fun part of the year. This is generally because the Sun occupies Cancer up until the 23rd and increases your power to enjoy and give enjoyment to other people. Further, it increases creative ambition and is likely to bring success to the artistic fish.

If you are a parent you will have good reason to feel proud of your offspring. And regardless of the weather it is an ideal time for escaping routine, perhaps in order to take a short break.

Where work is concerned, the aesthetic side to your character is enhanced, and should you use this in a professional capacity you can be sure of a good and positive month.

Romantically, Venus and Mercury join the Sun for the majority of the month. Venus will be encouraging a love of change and interesting intellectual pursuits, and you will be seeing the fascinating potential in literally everybody you meet. This planet will also be helping you to enjoy life and will help you to express yourself on a deep, emotional level. Love affairs may be pleasant although casual, and you can certainly gain through entertainment if this is your area of work.

Pisces is one of the mutable signs – the others being Sagittarius, Gemini and Virgo – and although in theory you are supposed to be adaptable, when it comes to emotions, as a water sign, Pisces, you are inclined to be hyper-sensitive and intense. Luckily, the planets during July help to lighten you up quite considerably and this will prove invaluable – you will not be taking yourself quite so seriously. So give yourself over to enjoyment but don't create any vast problems that cannot be solved at a later date.

That sexy, aggressive, power-driven planet Mars will be moving into Libra on the 21st of the month. Because of this you are unlikely to take any pressure from bureaucrats, officials and the like without defending yourself vigorously. You are no longer the timid fish who can be pushed from pillar to post, and your courageous new approach is likely to reap untold benefits.

Workwise, Jupiter is in retrograde action. Therefore, this is not a time for pushing ahead with ambitions. Rather, this placing suggests that it is necessary to retrace your steps before you can progress any further. It is a good time, too, for making plans of a professional nature. Soon life will be opening up where work matters are concerned, and if you are unemployed you will be able to secure long-term employment in the not too distant future. You have a great deal to look forward to.

Financially, Venus in the sign of Cancer implies certain fluctuations, and you need to ensure that you have sufficient funds in the bank before you impulsively write cheques. Some of you may gain from speculating although this is not recommended for every member of this sign. Certainly, if you have a little bit of spare cash and can afford to lose it, then enjoy yourself, but do not use your food money in the hope that you can solve pressing financial problems.

Healthwise, it is not surprising that with so much activity going on, both socially and perhaps on the sporting level, you begin to run out of energy on the

26th. Take the last five days of this month to rest and slow down.

Finally, as Saturn moves into retrograde movement on the 6th of the month and continues to wend its way through your sign, you would be most ill-advised to take on added responsibility as it would entail a great deal of work with precious little reward.

You have a great deal to look forward to this month. Try to enjoy every single moment in order to prepare yourself to take on board the more serious aspects of life later on in the year.

This month the full Moon occurs in the sign of Capricorn on the 12th. During this period you will be wise to double-check any social arrangements you may have with friends – they could prove to be unusual, although this may be due to circumstances beyond their control.

The new Moon this month occurs on the 27th July, in the sign of Leo. Because of this you may suddenly discover a need to learn a new technique, and it is also a time when job interviews can be especially successful. Those of you who are already employed are likely to discover increased activity at work and there may even be new members of staff – in which case, extend the hand of friendship. As always, new Moons can be used for making fresh starts, and this one is no exception.

AUGUST

This is a month when the stars are setting you a further lesson to learn – as mentioned in the general look at the year ahead. However, a reminder will do no harm.

It appears that you have now learnt how to establish yourself on all levels: spiritually, mentally, emotionally and physically. Apparently you have come to realize that it is necessary to be more scrupulous when dealing with financial matters – gone are the days when you tended to stick your head in the sand at the mention of the word 'money'.

Now you need to work on perpetuating your relationships. When you do you will discover this can be a real source of power. Furthermore, your attitude towards other people's resources is also likely to be changing at this time.

Saturn continues in your sign but regrettably is in retrograde action until next month. Therefore, during August you should decline any chance to take on board more responsibility. This is the last thing you need: it would only make you anxious and encourage negative thinking, which has a nasty habit of bringing about that which you most fear.

For the majority of the month the Sun will be squatting in the sign of Leo and you will be enjoying a certain amount of pride in all your achievements. You will be ambitious to serve and help other people and this is likely to be much appreciated by those closest to you. Healthwise, you are full of vitality and may even develop an interest in diet, hygiene or other keep-fit pursuits. Those of you who are in positions of power or influence will find that employed subordinates are both helpful and congenial.

August is an ideal time for those in the service industries and the medical profession and if you work in a freelance capacity or represent other people in the form, perhaps, of an agent or manager. Regardless of your profession you will be achieving a great deal of harmony between yourself and workmates.

Romantically, if you are fancy-free many of you will experience a temporary infatuation with somebody connected directly or indirectly with your work. However, it would not be a good idea to allow yourself to become too carried away: this is likely to be a temporary infatuation and one which you should enjoy rather than tormenting yourself as to the outcome.

From the 10th onwards Mercury moves into your opposite sign of Virgo. Once this occurs you will seek not only physical attraction but also intellectual compatibility. Many of you may be drawn to those who are younger or perhaps more intelligent – luckily Pisces is not a sign overloaded with ego problems. In all your relationships there is likely to be a restless and changeable theme, which will prove to be enjoyable and stimulating.

Jupiter finally resumes direct movement on the 22nd and from here on professional matters can be furthered providing you are prepared to take the initiative. Recent muddles, confusions and lack of progress evaporate and you begin to feel more at ease in this area of life.

Healthwise, the position of Venus in Leo up until the 23rd is likely to encourage the self-indulgent side to your character. However, many of you may decide that the price is worth paying, even if it means the occasional stomach upset or hangover. This aside there should be little to affect your physical wellbeing.

Also during August, Pluto will be resuming direct movement. You will find that where there was once aggravation and irritation from official sources you now seem able to retain the peace, perhaps by coming up with a realistic plan which is acceptable to all concerned.

Romantically, the best period is during the last week of the month when Venus enters your opposite sign of Virgo. Once this occurs, a rosy glow will appear over existing relationships and many of you may be tempted to 'name the day'. Should you be completely fancy-free during this period, take a second look at new members of the opposite sex with whom you are keeping company: amongst the many faces there is likely to be someone really worthwhile.

In the main August looks to be an extremely positive month with a great deal to look forward to; therefore, allow that self-confidence of yours free expression.

The full Moon this month occurs in the sign of Aquarius on the 10th, and because of this you may experience feelings of insecurity and inferiority. This is, of course, the negative side to the Piscean personality. But, hopefully, now that you have been made aware of the fact you will not take yourself too seriously. Use your time well, cram it full of activity and, above all else, make plans for the future, although without acting for the moment.

The new Moon occurs on the 26th in the sign of Virgo. It strongly suggests an important new relationship, and one that will occupy your life for some time to come. Alternatively, it may be that you are now prepared to take a romance that little step further and commitments could be made. Regardless of whether they are single or married, around this time all Pisceans will be meeting new and exciting people who will have a profound effect on their life.

SEPTEMBER

Because of the position of the Sun in your opposite sign of Virgo up until the 24th, you will be taking a great deal of pride in your own achievements and will also be drawn to other people more than usual. It is a rare fish who is of an independent disposition, but this is heightened during this particular September. Therefore, wherever possible try to work in harness or in partnership. Many of you will be experiencing a certain amount of satisfaction in your relationships with others and it is likely that you and your opposite number will be laying down ambitious plans for the future. The more you try and cooperate at this time the more beneficial September is likely to be. Clearly, then, an ideal time for those who work in a professional partnership for your ability to give and take will be reciprocated.

Romantically, the best period during September will be the first sixteen days, when Venus will occupy your opposite sign of Virgo. This will throw a rosy glow over all personal issues, and problems can be resolved by a certain amount of communication. Other people will be generous with their affections and you will respond accordingly. Furthermore, you couldn't have a better time if you are considering forming a professional relationship or joining a team.

Mercury's placing in Libra suggests that you may be developing a talent for research and analysis which will provide you with an insight into many situations, both of a professional and personal nature. However, where cash matters are concerned, there is a degree of inconsistency and you should try to conserve wherever possible.

Because Mercury goes into retrograde movement on the 22nd of the month, and from our position in space appears to be moving backwards, it is imperative that you arrange important meetings, negotiations and job interviews before this date as life can certainly become complicated under such an aspect.

During this month you will develop a wonderful ability to pacify and win over enemies and competitors. Few can resist you at this moment in time, Pisces, and you must push into life confidently with your head held high.

That aggressive and sexy planet Mars moves into the sign of Scorpio on the 7th, encouraging independence of thought and a tendency to fight for your convictions. A strong emphasis is likely to be placed on an unusual desire for change.

Financially it is likely that you can gain through foreign connections, higher education and legal matters.

On a personal level, it is imperative that you do not confuse love with sex. Physical attractions are likely to crop up out of the blue, and with those who would not normally appeal to you. Never mind, instead of lying awake at nights chewing your finger nails down to your elbows, why don't you simply lighten up, play safe and relax.

Luckily Saturn has now resumed direct movement; therefore, any responsibility which you are asked to take on board from here on in is likely to bring its own reward in the fullness of time. Furthermore, you can also benefit from the experiences of wiser and older heads. Try to be less secretive and more confiding and you will find your progress considerably smoothed during the month ahead.

During September there will be a natural inclination to become suddenly interested in a myriad different pastimes. However, try not to spread your energies too thinly otherwise you will make little progress. Concentrate them more and you will derive the maximum amount of enjoyment.

The full Moon during September falls in your own sign on the 9th during this 24-hour period. You will need to dredge out your sense of humour and adopt a caring attitude to yourself as you are likely to suffer from unrealistic feelings of insecurity. This is mainly because your feelings are prominent and that active imagination of yours is running away with itself. As is invariably the case, this is an ideal time for making plans and if you can keep your head busy in this direction, perhaps you will be able to avoid this pitfall.

The new Moon during September occurs in the sign of Virgo on the 24th. This is, of course, your opposite sign and therefore represents either a new partnership of a professional nature or, indeed, a personal one. Certainly popularity will be hitting an all-time high and you are more responsive to the feelings and thoughts of other people at this time. As with all new Moons this is an excellent time for making fresh starts, particularly where the personal side of life is concerned. Forge ahead, banish all negative feelings or thoughts of failure and you can make this period one which will be remembered for quite some time.

OCTOBER

Up until the 24th the Sun will be squatting in the sign of Libra. This will increase your awareness of higher forces and you are also likely to be intent on self-improvement. This is a time, too, when you will find it a great deal easier to recruit other people to support you in one way or another.

Mercury finally resumes direct movement on the 14th. Not only will this increase any natural talent for research or analysis but it will also give you an insight into some important situation and help you to progress where travel, legal matters or job interviews are concerned, providing you arrange them after this date. You are also likely to meet an above average number of unusual but interesting people and they will spark off your imagination. However, it might be a good idea to consciously avoid becoming involved with too many cranks, despite the fact that they may amuse you.

Venus will be moving into the sign of Scorpio on the 10th, encouraging your already considerable amount of creative inspiration, sympathy, understanding and intuition. Those of you who deal with foreigners or foreign matters will find this a pleasant time and many of you could become romantically involved with people from very different backgrounds. For some while now you may have been considering enrolling in a course of learning. This could be anything from a new diet or health regime to the study of foreign philosophies: whichever applies you will certainly be shining and deriving a great deal of satisfaction.

Mars continues to wend its way through Scorpio until the 21st. Such a placing encourages independent thought, which is no bad thing for an indecisive Pisces. Too often you tend to rely on other people, but not so right now. You will be fighting for your beliefs and convictions with a fervour which will be much admired. But it is possible that you may sometimes develop a love of change for its own sake.

Once Mars moves into Sagittarius on the 21st the desire for conquest will be strong. You will possess inexhaustible energy where your career is concerned, but must guard against taking too much. However, you will be resolute and independent and will find success through enterprise. Luckily this is also a time when you will be living very firmly in the present rather than dwelling on past mistakes or wistfully looking towards the future and what might be.

Regardless of what you do for a living you will be putting your heart and soul into it. On occasions you may believe that you are inexhaustible but then, to your surprise, you will suddenly fall by the wayside. In order to achieve a proper balance be sure that you get sufficient rest periods and there will be little you cannot accomplish this month. You can also rest assured that any extra effort you put in on behalf of other people or work will be well rewarded in the future. Should you experience any doubt about your direction in life turn to your male friends for advice and this applies to both men and women.

There will also be an inclination to become physically involved with people you meet whilst going about your professional duties, and just for once you will not be looking for Romeo or Juliet but simply gratifying your physical appetite.

Now that your ruling planet Neptune resumes direct movement on the 5th, your progress will be considerably accelerated for the remainder of the year. Instead of experiencing that feeling of one step forward and six steps back, the road ahead now seems clear and you feel confident that you can achieve your heart's desire, and you will be right.

October certainly seems to be a constructive, positive and rewarding period and you must do all in your power to extract the most out of it.

But one word of warning. If you are a family person, because of your increased concentration on external matters those at home may accuse you of neglect. Although it may be difficult, strive to balance your life a little more evenly and the entire month should be satisfying in all areas.

The full Moon this month occurs in the sign of Aries on the 8th, signalling a period when extra vigilance where cash is concerned will certainly pay off: money seems to come and go rather easily at this time. Avoid making any kind of commitment, particularly to long-term payments. The 8th is also an excellent day for making plans for your financial future, which you can put into operation very soon.

The new Moon occurs on the 24th in the sign of Scorpio. This will help to sharpen your already receptive and imaginative mind and will further underscore your sincere beliefs, no matter what they may be. Chances to travel should be snapped up, and any new people you meet are likely to be worthwhile, either on a material or perhaps an emotional basis. As always, you can use this period for beginning fresh work, meeting new people and generally preparing to start anew.

NOVEMBER

For the majority of this month, the Sun will be squatting in the watery sign of Scorpio, encouraging high idealism, a love of travel, and an interest in foreigners' and other people's little idiosyncracies, as well as introducing a broad wisdom to your every thought and action. Those of you who work abroad or in connection with legal matters and higher education should certainly be in for a productive and rewarding time.

Mercury, too, will be occupying the sign of Scorpio between the 4th and the 23rd. Should you possess talent for research or analysis this will definitely be increased and encouraged at this time. Furthermore, you will be developing an insight into problems that have been hanging around for some time and clearing the decks in order to start over again.

November tends to be a remarkable month from the astrological point of view as there are no less than four planets situated in the sign of Sagittarius, the area of your life devoted to work. It is not difficult, then, to decide exactly where your priorities will lie during this time. The position of the Sun in this sign shows that you will be strongly self-conscious but determined to achieve. Success is likely to come your way and many of you will acquire a high position; others will find it relatively easy to find patronage and support.

Mars in the same sign as the Sun will develop anew an uncharacteristic desire for conquest. When it comes to work you are inexhaustible but you must take care not to attempt too much. In the main you will be independent, resolute and successful through enterprise. Furthermore, you will be inclined to live in the present rather than the future or the past. Professionally you are in for a lively, interesting and active time. However, Mars can create a certain amount of bad feeling: try to avoid being too pushy otherwise you may upset workmates and develop potential enemies. However, if you can retain some of that Piscean charm you will have little to worry about.

Venus also occupies the sign of Sagittarius between the 3rd and the 28th. This is good news for those of you in creative work, and pleasant experiences as well as a certain amount of socializing will be in progress in connection with all professional matters. Many of you will find great success, even honour, and everyone will benefit from the insight of women.

If you are fancy-free the presence of Venus, the planet of love, and Mars, the planet of sex, in the same sign seems to suggest that you could be meeting someone very special in connection with your professional duties. Don't make the mistake of thinking this is simply a flirtation which will pass swiftly; as the weeks draw into months you will come to realize that you are involved in something really meaningful. Apart from the strong attraction which seems to exist between you, many common interests will help to perpetuate the relationship.

However, if you are already in a relationship or married, your loved ones may feel that you are neglecting them. Should this be the case it might be necessary to try and balance your life a little more evenly, for all work and no play is sure to wreak havoc with your personal life.

It is an exceptionally lucky time if you are self-employed or in positions of power or authority. You will be making good and incisive decisions on behalf of yourself and your company. Many of you will be learning of some long-overdue promotion, whilst those Pisceans who are out of work are likely to land a lucrative job — assuming, of course, that you have not already given up. Hopefully this does not apply, but if it does you get up and prepare to fight another day.

Certainly where your professional wishes and desires are concerned, you could not have a better planetary set-up, and it is up to you to push ahead rather than waiting on other people to give you directives or encouragement. Self-motivation should be your motto throughout this month if you are to make the most of it.

Financially, it is unlikely that you will receive anything for nothing, although monies owed for past efforts will certainly come rolling in.

Saturn continues in your sign and once it returns to direct movement after the 21st it is likely that many of you will be asked to take on board fresh responsibility. Should this opportunity arise you must be ready to grab it with both hands: just for once play the orange sunflower and not the shrinking violet. If ever there was a time for drawing attention to your myriad talents this is it, Pisces; do not waste these ensuing few weeks.

Healthwise, you need to be sure that you get at least one early night each week if you are to cope efficiently with all that life will be demanding of you. Armed with this advice there is nothing you cannot achieve and it is very much a case of 'best foot forwards'. Provided you don't allow anybody or anything to deflect you from your purpose, this will be the most productive month you have experienced for quite some time.

The Moon is full in the sign of Taurus on the 7th and denotes a period when you will be easily swayed by your own environment and could be unusually impressionable, dreamy and moody. Luckily you will be adaptable but, nevertheless, this is not a time for important moves; rather, one for laying down a blueprint for the rest of your life.

The new Moon during November occurs on the 22nd in the sign of Scorpio, and there is likely be an opportunity to go on a short trip, perhaps for professional reasons. You will be impressionable and your imagination will run riot, but in a practical way. But your beliefs are sincere and those around will be impressed by your positive frame of mind. As is always the case, new Moons can be utilized for meeting fresh faces, visiting new places and generally making new starts. This is a wonderful month, Pisces; be sure you do not waste a moment of it.

DECEMBER

Although some of the emphasis continues to be on work there seems to be a less frantic atmosphere now because Mars has moved into the sign of Capricon, where it will be joined by Mercury after the 12th of the month.

During early December your determination to find success as well as promotion continues. Furthermore, you will be using your knowledge profitably and your adaptability will certainly be helping your career. The first couple of weeks of the month are great for commercial success and for those involved in the literary world or travel. Minor changes of direction at work will be beneficial and you must be ready to consider them seriously. Many new people and contacts will be entering your life in this area.

After the 12th, Mercury will join Mars in the sign of Capricorn and there will be no less than five planets in this sign. The Sun will be encouraging your social ambitions although it is likely that ulterior motives

are at work here. Nevertheless, you will find it easier
to cooperate successfully with everyone, both in your
personal and professional life. In the former you will
find yourself more popular and in a position to influence
friends. Mars' placing in Capricon seems to indicate
that your desires are increasing and your wishes more
powerful, and there will be an uncharacteristic tendency for you to take the lead where social life is
concerned. Because of this you will be making many
casual acquaintances – and these fresh faces are likely
to belong to enterprising and energetic people.

With both Venus and Mars in the area of your chart
devoted to friendship, you are sure to be deriving a
great deal of happiness and contentment from friends,
contacts and acquaintances. You are most likely to be
drawn to the more cultured and artistic in your close
circle and will be socializing a great deal more than
usual.

Romantically, although you are unlikely to be riding
on cloud nine, those you are attracted to will not only be
providing you with a strong sexual, and even emotional,
pull but are also likely to end up as friends for life once
the infatuation has died away. Never mind, Pisces, our
friends are frequently with us a great deal longer than
husbands, wives, or even lovers.

Those of you who rely strongly on contacts for professional advancement, such as freelance workers, will
certainly be doing well this month, and the more you
can combine business with pleasure the more success
you will find.

Healthwise, there may be a slight tendency to exhaustion during the first twelve days but providing you
get in at least a couple of early nights you will be
able to handle everything with a certain expertise and
panache.

Strangely enough, although this month contains the

festive period, matters related to home and domesticity seem to be temporarily ignored. It seems that your mind is on ambitions and potential achievements rather than matters related to family or relatives. So don't be surprised if there are a few complaints later on in the month by which time you are sure to be ready to listen and acquiesce.

A word of warning: Venus will enter the sign of Aquarius on the 22nd and this will quieten you down considerably. You will become more intuitive, perceptive and contemplative, and the secretive side to your character will be resurrected. Certainly you will be feeling charitable and unselfish, but this gentle and emotional mood could lead you into temptation where romance is concerned. You would be well advised to proceed carefully and be on the lookout for a degree of deception. Of course, it may be you who is perpetrating this state of affairs, in which case the choice is entirely up to you. However, take care that you do not play your own worst enemy.

The full Moon this month occurs on the 7th in the sign of Gemini. It seems to suggest discontent and difficulty on the home front which, when we take into consideration the above tendencies, is hardly surprising. Take care that around the full Moon differences do not assume tremendous proportions. Try to sweeten the bitter pill which you are expecting relatives to swallow by going out of your way to be particularly attentive around this period, otherwise you could be leaving yourself wide open to criticism and difficulty. This, as usual, is avoidable.

The new Moon during December occurs on the 22nd in the sign of Sagittarius. Once more the emphasis seems to be on ambition and professional matters. If you are combining business with pleasure during this period you will be making many interesting contacts, but may also become detrimentally involved with a colleague. Providing you can maintain an open stance where this relationship is concerned you will be able to side-step any potentially difficult situations. Be carefree and flirty but be sure that others do not misinterpret your intentions. You will end the year full of optimism and, hopefully, a good deal richer.

Daily Guide

JANUARY

SUNDAY 1st Today there is a new Moon, and it occurs in the sign of Capricorn. This means it will be filling you with optimism and positive thinking for the year ahead. Today the actions of a close friend will make you realize that it is not what you have in this life that counts but those who occupy an important part in it.

MONDAY 2nd As a Piscean you are never motivated by ambition or greed. In fact, right now there is a wonderful feeling of gentle serenity and sensitivity, and because of this you need to spend your time with those who appreciate you best.

TUESDAY 3rd It seems that the course of the planets has set you the job of swimming upstream. This is usually the case, but right now even more so – and, in fact, it is the only way you will ever find lasting happiness or peace.

WEDNESDAY 4th This is an ideal time to become part of a team, to join forces and achieve your ends through joint effort. Easier said than done, however, for your nature and personality is much too fluid to work in complete harmony with go-getters; they simply don't have your perception, intuition and creative abilities.

Nevertheless, look around for the right person, they are sure to be within your sights.

THURSDAY 5th The Moon is in your sign today and it seems to suggest that if you put your mind to it you can make great strides by allowing others to lead the way and guide you in the right direction. The truth of this statement is borne out by the fact that Pluto is now at the zenith of your chart, where it highlights good luck and eventual promotion.

FRIDAY 6th You are in a reflective mood and should bear in mind that the individual talents given to us at birth shine forth only when encouraged, and that the conscious, careful selection of the activities, situations or people to whom we devote our time and attention is all that separates serene and contented people from those who are unhappy.

SATURDAY 7th The reflective mood of yesterday continues and is encouraged by the fact that Mercury is now in the area of your chart devoted to intuition, withdrawal and contemplation. However, because this placing will last for several weeks it will be necessary to force yourself to join in with what is happening around you: isolation certainly won't help you get what you want out of life.

SUNDAY 8th Venus moves to the zenith of your chart, encouraging good fortune, harmony and the chance to excel yourself on the work front. Although today is Sunday it might be a good idea to get in touch with colleagues, particularly if you believe you have any good, creative ideas.

MONDAY 9th Ruled by Neptune, you are inclined to have a great deal in common with the other water signs,

Cancer and Scorpio: you all reach out with open arms to protect, provide and pamper the object of your affection. And certainly the position of the Moon in Taurus right now is encouraging you to be more adventurous in the personal side to life.

TUESDAY 10th The stars today associate themselves with things that are mysterious and ephemeral. Now the time has arrived to place even greater value on yourself, your diet and your physical wellbeing. Should you have experienced exhaustion and its side effects this is an ideal time for medical and dental check ups. These will help to ensure a healthy 1995.

WEDNESDAY 11th Today is the time for backing your image with courage and enthusiasm. If you want to make changes then do so, and feel the reality of your new self. Live in the expectancy of greater things to come – and your subconscious will help them to materialize.

THURSDAY 12th You are now given the opportunity to walk away from what is stopping you from living life to the fullest extent. You must be seen and accepted for what you are rather than for the way others imagine or want you to be.

FRIDAY 13th The Moon in Gemini today will be stirring up action within the family. However, refuse to allow yourself to be threatened or brow-beaten into accepting the values or ambitions of other people. You have your own life to lead and must remember this.

SATURDAY 14th Today Venus is in a beautiful aspect with Jupiter at the zenith of your chart and this planetary action is trying to make you realize that it will soon be time to break the habit of a lifetime and use your gifts to broaden your mental horizon. Take up new challenges and stop turning everything inwards. Basically, start 'going for it'.

SUNDAY 15th The Moon in Cancer provides you with a light-hearted day and one when you need to let off steam in physical activities such as sports, or simply relax in company with close friends. Romance has a flirty feel about it, too, and you should accept all chances of pleasure which come your way at this moment in time.

MONDAY 16th The full Moon in the sign of Cancer could make young people in your life difficult; therefore, if you have children you will need to be firm but gentle. A creative project may take longer to get of the ground than you envisaged. Never mind, providing you remain persistent you will achieve your goals in the end.

TUESDAY 17th Today, it is most important to be grateful you were born with a questioning mind – and to aspire to something better and finer. Those who are currently giving you a hard time over money have no real conception of what life is all about, their eyes are blinkered.

WEDNESDAY 18th You must resolve to be more independent: stand on your own two feet and knock on doors till the right one opens. Any challenging aspects during the month ahead cannot thwart, harm or tame you if, as the adage goes, 'you keep your eye on the doughnut and not on the hole'.

THURSDAY 19th Today Pluto moves to the zenith of your chart into the sign of Sagittarius, the planet of regeneration and rebirth. It also suggests that your professional potential is unlimited; aspire to the heights and believe in your abilities, taste and judgements. Perceive and imagine what you wish to be, keep that thought in mind and push ahead, with everything on your list of priorities.

FRIDAY 20th If you are to attain your desires it may necessitate an unusual amount of travelling in the near future, and this could result in relatives and colleagues feeling resentful at being left to their own devices. Be that as it may, the call will be much too powerful to resist.

SATURDAY 21st The Sun today moves into the sign of Aquarius and you are provided with a couple of weeks which should be spent in self-examination and trying to establish in your own mind exactly what direction you want to be travelling in six months hence. Don't rush into a decision, take your time, and once you have arrived at the right course of action implement your plans and stick to them with tenacity. Use this period for contemplation.

SUNDAY 22nd The Moon in Libra today will make it difficult for you to completely turn off ambitions or work matters. And it is likely that you will be spending a considerable amount of time either on the phone or in the company of colleagues. Possibly your family will not be best pleased, and although it would be a good idea to explain yourself, in no way should you try to justify time spent in this way.

MONDAY 23rd Mars moves into the sign of Leo today, making it likely that over the next few weeks or so the pace will be hotting up on the professional front. You will exhaust easily if you insist on burning the candle at both ends. Ensure that you set aside periods for real relaxation or you could miss out on some of the action and, as a result, the fruits of your labours, too.

TUESDAY 24th   Today the Moon is in the water sign of Scorpio, which is, of course, compatible with you. Expectation is the key to motivation: remember that the winners in this life are not only dissatisfied with the status quo but also want to change the world or their situations for the better. In other words, do not moan about a set of circumstances, be prepared to act.

WEDNESDAY 25th   Being born under the modest sign of Pisces you have considerably more going for you than you realize, and all you really have to do is keep thinking on simple lines. There are times when you live like a recluse, depending on your moods: often you are on the shore of reality, but sometimes in the sea of imagination.

THURSDAY 26th   Today the emphasis is on pleasure, romance, sports and entertaining. This is a time to cast away any problems that may be bothering you and totally relax. If you are spending time in the company of children you will find them amusing as well as entertaining – a light-hearted day.

FRIDAY 27th   The Moon at the zenith point of your chart is encouraging you to make the necessary changes which will speed up your progress and help to achieve your ambitions in life. Should you be unemployed, this is an ideal time for looking for work. Put out a few feelers; the opportunities are there, all you need to do is locate them.

SATURDAY 28th   As a Piscean you are acutely aware of your own moods, of your need for inner life or life in the world, to be private or in a relationship. Whether you are shining and light-hearted or withdrawn and secretive, you will dance in tune with the music of the planets over this weekend.

SUNDAY 29th   The Moon in Capricorn will certainly liven up your life today and new contacts will inspire you and spur you on to greater things in the future. Should you visit a club it is likely you will run into exciting new people – extend the hand of friendship rather than being withdrawn.

MONDAY 30th   The new Moon in Aquarius today will sharpen your instincts and it is up to you to have the confidence to rely on them. Whenever you go against your 'gut feeling' you invariably live to regret it, don't you?

TUESDAY 31st   You are at your most creative and inspired right now, do not waste time in reflection or isolation; push yourself out into life and make a conscientious effort to make some of your wistful dreams come true.

FEBRUARY

WEDNESDAY 1st   The Moon in your sign will certainly increase your confidence; however, in a good relationship both parties learn to give and take without complaint, and now you need to listen attentively and not set yourself up as judge and jury. There are many problems that need to be resolved but not one of them is as important as your ability to find the right solution.

THURSDAY 2nd   Because you are at your most sensitive this is an ideal day for leaving your options open and doing everything you can to ease existing stress in partnership affairs. Cashwise, unless you make certain concessions and adjustments others may gain the upper hand. Pluto and Sagittarius urge you to look beyond professional conflicts and arguments and not let false pride stop you from being sympathetic, magnanimous and generous.

FRIDAY 3rd   Where professional business contacts or relationships are concerned you appear to have reached an interesting phase and even, perhaps, breaking point. If you take your mind back to late last year you will understand why a final showdown or confrontation is inevitable.

SATURDAY 4th   The Sun is in a beautiful aspect to Mercury today in that very private and secretive part of your chart. Time, then, to keep a low profile, make plans and recall where you have gone wrong in the past where ambitions are concerned. The chances are you will realize that you may have failed because of a lack of 'follow through', and are now vowing that this will not happen again.

SUNDAY 5th   Venus moves into Capricorn, bringing a certain amount of goodwill, warmth and generosity from your friendship circle. Those of you who are self-employed or in freelance work can be sure that over the next few weeks contacts and acquaintances will be only too glad to help out in any way they can – all you have to do is ask.

MONDAY 6th   Today Mercury is in beautiful aspect with Jupiter, and other people are generous and open-minded as well as lucky for you. Therefore, do not isolate yourself from the real world; be prepared to work alongside others and in this way you can make the most of your talents and find success.

TUESDAY 7th   Right now you can put a proposal or project together that will placate those who have had you on the run recently. In fact, planetary activity must increase your bargaining power in both personal and career issues. Remember that a cycle or chapter in your life is possibly now coming to a close.

WEDNESDAY 8th   Circumstances today are encouraging you to confront emotional or partnership problems head-on, and to make others understand they are living in a fantasy world. Events which took place in December made your position clear, but you probably believed companions would eventually come to their senses. They haven't, and you must now think of your own comfort, happiness and security.

THURSDAY 9th   The Moon in Gemini seems to suggest that it would be a good idea to rebuild and replan life. You must stop hankering after times gone by or what you consider to be 'the golden, olden days'. Recent aspects suggest that with a fresh approach and greater self-confidence you can survive this emotionally demanding phase and benefit from past experience.

FRIDAY 10th   The Moon in Gemini suggests that a fresh approach to domestic or property affairs could

turn around a potentially difficult situation. Those of
you who plan to entertain visitors this evening need to
get yourself organized in order to avert a muddling and
chaotic time, which would not make a good impression.
A little bit of thought will take you a long way.

SATURDAY 11th　A day and, in fact, a weekend for
sheer pleasure and enjoyment. Sporting events are
stimulating and lucky for you and party-going will
provide you with the opportunity to socialize and meet
new people. You are at your most flirty – so Heaven
help the opposite sex.

SUNDAY 12th　It is imperative that you do not make
promises to other people which you will find difficult
to fulfil in the near future, otherwise your reputation
of being a 'no hoper' will be enhanced and this could
backfire on you, perhaps on a professional level. Say
what you mean and mean what you say.

MONDAY 13th　Today it looks as if other people hold
the trump card as far as cash matters are concerned, and
you may well be pressured into forgoing certain rights
or claims. The whole matter may seem unjust but you
are now competing with people who seem to be devoid
of any scruples. Your best course of action is to simply
close the door on the past and look to the future.

TUESDAY 14th　If ever there was a time to change your
approach and look beyond petty bigotry, this must be
it. Therefore, get on your broomstick and don't permit
anyone – no matter how close to you or how important
they have been in the past – to influence your judgement
or cramp your style.

WEDNESDAY 15th　Today is the day of the full Moon
and you could find workmates and colleagues, as well

as business contacts, a little out of sorts. They seem to be much preoccupied with their own problems, and because of this seem uncooperative. The best thing to do is to leave them to their own devices whilst you get on with what needs to be done.

THURSDAY 16th There are certain situations you cannot change and these are people who will never admit that they are at fault or consider they have broken a rule. No amount of argument, emotional conflict or criticism can stop you from pushing ahead with a major alteration in the pattern of your working life.

FRIDAY 17th Today Venus is in a beautiful aspect to responsible Saturn. This will have a steadying effect on your emotions and there may be constructive financial gains. An excellent day too for putting cash affairs on a more reliable basis. A relationship with a much older person seems to be emphasized; this may be romantic, but not necessarily so.

SATURDAY 18th Mercury resumes movement today. You have been cramped where travel matters, documents, job interviews and meetings are concerned; you will now be able to push ahead in these areas. Indeed, the stars are encouraging you to do so. Those closest to you will be far more cooperative than they have been for quite some while now.

SUNDAY 19th The Sun today moves into your sign, flooding you with solar power, confidence and a feeling of wellbeing. You begin a period of forging ahead and should do so with courage and optimism. The more positive you can be the more success you are likely to glean.

MONDAY 20th Although it may still be some time before a financial or professional matter is settled to your satisfaction, you should now be back on form and living up to your reputation of being level-headed. Do, however, take others' tokens of affection, respect and admiration seriously.

TUESDAY 21st If you are still trying to negotiate terms, or imagine you are being taken for a ride, then you haven't profited from Pluto's move into Sagittarius. But by rights you ought now to be so involved with new schemes and projects that you no longer care about others' lack of understanding and integrity or anyone's attempts to score points.

WEDNESDAY 22nd One of the great things about astrology is that new planetary aspects are always being formed. Therefore, no matter how difficult a situation, the pain and problems always pass. After all the heartaches and anguish of the recent past you should certainly be on the mend now, building bridges and taking a more positive view of personal and cash matters.

THURSDAY 23rd Although it is rare for lightning to strike twice, it seems you are in a similar position to the one you were in six months ago. This time, however, you really can force the pace, make a number of decisive actions, and experience the excitement and personal success you have always known was possible.

FRIDAY 24th Regardless of your age or circumstances, there is a more exciting and fuller life to be lived. Even if you have to pick up sticks, make some kind of financial settlement during the next few weeks or so: rarely will you have felt so on the ball and on the right track.

SATURDAY 25th   The aspects in operation today are the kind which will remove restrictions, and even if you are still smarting from criticism recently received from a long-term connection or companion, you still ought to be planning to blaze a number of new trails now.

SUNDAY 26th   Venus is in a beautiful aspect to your ruling planet Neptune, and this will be encouraging happiness of the most enduring kind and can bring platonic friendships with real depth, understanding and feeling. The influence will refine your feelings and promote emotional maturity, taking you to a more advanced level. It is also indicative of a blissfully romantic time and one which you will look back on with a certain amount of nostalgia.

MONDAY 27th   Developments which have taken place in your personal life and affairs over recent months are probably a prelude to what is promised this year. If you are ready to alter your stance over home, property and family matters, you will experience a rare kind of inner serenity and peace – a time for personal achievement.

TUESDAY 28th   Venus is in wonderful aspect to Uranus today and this seems to make for a memorable social life and good all round conditions. The time is now right for change, and this is sure to be a positive period: be ready to take advantage.

MARCH

WEDNESDAY 1st   The new Moon today suggests that you make the most of this time in order to allow the world to see just how adventurous and inspired you really are. You are now in a strong enough position to capitalize on your creative talents. What occurs both now and during the next couple of days will leave you breathless but bathed in personal glory, and you will wonder why you ever doubted your own ability to succeed.

THURSDAY 2nd Regardless of where you happen to be this should be a time of renewed optimism: enjoy each new experience. During the past couple of months there have been times when a series of battles has coincided with forced changes, both in your personal life and at work. You really deserve a break.

FRIDAY 3rd Today Venus enters the sign of Aquarius suggesting it is time to turn off the charm and turn on the pressure. Certain people will not respond to the gentle approach and you are entitled to know exactly where you stand. Don't expect to finalize a cash settlement without having to modify your claims or make the odd concession.

SATURDAY 4th Pluto's retrograde action suggests that you turn your mind back to less fortunate times and analyse your responses to current changes either at home or at work. It is possible that everything may seem out of control, but in actual fact you have reached a major turning point and have a marvellous chance to live a more comfortable and contented existence.

SUNDAY 5th This is a time for considering entering new agreements or forming new relationships. Should you do so, by the middle part of the year you should have totally reorganized your domestic life. Use this period and the first few weeks of July to the full. Chance meetings and encounters today could have an effect on the future direction of your life.

MONDAY 6th　You should not have time for remorse, only an intense desire to get back on an even keel and discover new ways to capitalize on your creative and artistic talents The breadth of your scope should be apparent today, but it is up to you to take the initiative and see the opportunities in even complex and supposedly difficult situations.

TUESDAY 7th　Try to decide what you really want rather than fantasizing about what you think you want. You will see the way ahead, but it will come to you in an inspired flash of lightning. Suddenly you will want to change so much because you will see a great deal that is restrictive and unnecessary, and even destructive. In every area there can no longer be hang-ups or hangers-on.

WEDNESDAY 8th　Mars today is in a beautiful aspect to Jupiter, and this supplies you with a couple of days in which you should seize cash opportunities and maybe even search around for ways to invest and make your money grow. Other people will be presenting you with money-making suggestions and it will be well worth taking a couple of days to think things through before turning them down.

THURSDAY 9th　This continues to be an excellent period for cash matters, and you should arrange to meet up with people who have an influence on this side to your life. Although you will be feeling lucky, on no account should you be tempted into speculations or gambling of any description.

FRIDAY 10th　Past emotional conflicts and separations may lead you to consider settling for second-best in order to avoid any more dramas. Well, you must put on a brave face, fight against the tide of opinion and do what you know needs to be done. It is likely that the direction you are following will be clearly signposted.

SATURDAY 11th New emotional attachments or ties seem to predominate in your chart and there seems to be a direct link between these and matters related to foreign or legal affairs. Today you must follow your own lucky star, even if long-standing associates label you selfish or self-indulgent.

SUNDAY 12th By nature you are a bit of a 'worry wart', but whatever your age or circumstances you must now think along more constructive and adventurous lines. Remember that no one is keeping score. By all means continue to do and give of your best, but if you do not enjoy being competitive, then change the rules and your approach to career matters.

MONDAY 13th The emphasis today is on pleasure, romance, sports and entertainments. This is a time to cast away any problems that may be bothering you and totally relax. If you are spending time in the company of children you will find them easy to handle.

TUESDAY 14th Today it is important to stand your ground and eliminate anything that is causing you heartache. The time has come to discard anything or anyone who no longer has a part in your long-term plans. However, you were born under one of the most sensitive signs of the zodiac and in certain areas are loath to break the habit of a life time. Unfortunately, now you must.

WEDNESDAY 15th It is likely you will be bitten by the travel bug today, and even if you are not travelling you could be making plans to do so in the not too distant future. Furthermore, there is a possibility that you will be able to embrace change once you have won over close companions or partners, who will need to be ready to take a great deal more on trust.

THURSDAY 16th Mercury moves into your sign and will liven up your entire personality. It will also provide you with a couple of weeks for making adjustments to plans as well as major changes. Many of you will be considering self-improvement, perhaps in the form of a new course of learning. Travel taken during this time will be lucky and enjoyable.

FRIDAY 17th The full Moon today occurs in your opposite sign of Virgo, and is likely to resurrect feelings within other people that may have been hidden for some while now. There is a possibility that you will be in for one or two surprises, or even shocks. However, this is not a time for issuing ultimatums; it would be better to lay down plans for the future though without acting for the time being.

SATURDAY 18th If you are criticized or attacked right now it might be a good idea to give in gracefully. You must understand that the problems which preoccupy so many of your friends and relatives are purely imaginary. You would do better to stick to interests that matter to you.

SUNDAY 19th It would be a wise move to listen to close partners right now. You should read between the lines instead of being taken in by their promises and claims. Luckily, Mercury in your sign will certainly sharpen your intellect and it is unlikely that others will find it as easy to take advantage of you as they normally do.

MONDAY 20th The Sun is in beautiful aspect to Uranus, providing you with an eventful and dynamic day. Relationships are emphasized – either their making or breaking. Financial gains are also a possibility, and you will be feeling more dynamic and outgoing. When it comes to socializing this evening you are likely to be drawn to those who are a little different, even downright eccentric.

TUESDAY 21st Today the Sun is in beautiful aspect to Pluto. There is a likelihood that cash matters will be emphasized and that you could begin a new phase of your life, perhaps a complete change of direction, though not without certain difficulties. Pluto's influence may be in evidence, perhaps encouraging you to begin fresh projects or bring unsatisfactory conditions to an end. Both will be good and positive.

WEDNESDAY 22nd Despite the fact that your chart is encouraging you to press on selfishly to develop your unique talents, the general feel for the day is slowly moving towards selflessness. If you are changing your job, go for something you really want.

THURSDAY 23rd There are indications today that changes are taking place at work. If you are to push through a major improvement which has been brewing for some time, you will have to make some commitments soon or you may miss out on the opportunity, and that would be a great pity.

FRIDAY 24th Your financial planet Mars has now resumed direct movement. Therefore, where money affairs are concerned your progress will be nothing short of startling over the next few weeks, or even months. A good time, too, for chasing that which is owed to you. Avoid the Piscean temptation to be soft-hearted and let other people off the hook.

SATURDAY 25th Mercury is in a beautiful aspect to Saturn today and this puts you in an overly-serious frame of mind. Keep yourself occupied and use this time for making decisions: unless you keep those grey cells busy you may find yourself sinking into a depression. But if you can fight this, much good and constructive work can be done in the way of problem solving. When it comes to your emotions, you are a good deal more steady than usual and will instinctively know what needs to be done.

SUNDAY 26th The time has arrived for some hard thinking and straight talking. Relatives or others that you may live with are likely to be both irritating and irritable. But whatever you do, don't allow yourself to be distracted or upset by harsh words – concentrate instead on getting to the truth and once you have made choices, put them into operation as soon as possible.

MONDAY 27th Everybody accepts the fact that you are a visionary, and for once the planets seem to agree with this. Make certain that relatives, partners and bosses are aware of your extraordinary ideas and, who knows, they might take you seriously for a change. You appear to be on to a real winner this time, and you should maximize your luck.

TUESDAY 28th Venus, the planet of love and creativity, enters your sign and will stay there over the next couple of weeks. Therefore, you should think less about making new friends and more about consolidating the feelings that you have recently developed. If you act fast, temporary relationships could become a permanent fixture.

WEDNESDAY 29th   It looks as though you are reaching a turning point in your life, and although a minor one it is only none the less fortunate. A series of cycles in your personal affairs seems to be taking up a great deal of your time and attention, but you must fight hard to concentrate on completing all unfinished business.

THURSDAY 30th   Mercury is in an out-of-the-world aspect with romantic Neptune. This provides a refining influence today and may lead to a need for peace and quiet, or even poetry, and this will certainly help to heighten your artistic sensitivity. It's a time, too, when new people will enter your life and they are likely to be important for some time to come. Romance is extremely well starred and there seems to be a coming together between yourself and other people.

FRIDAY 31st   The new Moon today falls in the financial area of life, promising a fresh source of money in the very near future. All opportunities that come in today should be snapped up without further ado, although you are advised to avoid any kind of gambling or speculating.

APRIL

SATURDAY 1st   You really seem to have the best of both worlds right now. You are at your most attractive and intelligent, and far more courageous than usual. Try to live up to the great expectations the planets seem to be offering you. Be sure that you boost your confidence and do whatever it takes to do so. Stop making excuses – push ahead.

SUNDAY 2nd Mercury is in a positive aspect with Pluto today and although this suggests inner battles, new looks may have to be developed and old ideas discarded. But the process will be less turbulent than it sounds. Luckily, now is the time for putting deep-rooted problems into perspective. This may be due to the fact that you are able to seek advice from someone close to you. Today also could lead to a complete change of attitude, either on the personal front or in your work.

MONDAY 3rd Because the Sun is lining up with Mars in a positive way, it is likely to be an extremely hard-working time. However, you do have abundant energy and it needs to be channelled in a positive way: events which occur today could affect the whole course of your life and this time will be remembered well into the future.

TUESDAY 4th For a person who is normally so private your chart is currently very public. You may well be more open about your feelings and desires, but perhaps not your intention. It seems as if you can't appreciate everyday life unless you can throw out a cloud of mystery.

WEDNESDAY 5th The Sun is in wonderful aspect to Jupiter today, and many astrologers believe this to be the best aspect. It is certainly a time when you will be able to reach your full potential and you will be stretching yourself in order to discover just what you are capable of. Financial and social affairs are also likely to prosper. This can be an extremely beneficial day and it should not go unnoticed. Push ahead with everything and anyone that is important to you.

THURSDAY 6th The Moon in Gemini puts you in a changeable mood: one moment you feel supremely confident, the next confused and bewildered. Despite this, it is a great time to make changes where professional matters are concerned. In your personal life, a distance which has grown up between you and someone else is about to be bridged.

FRIDAY 7th You appear to be looking far and wide for inspiration at this moment in time. Expect new stimulation and fresh responsibilities on the work front. It might also be a good idea to revive activities long left on the shelf. However, do steer clear of a possible clash with people in positions of power; it would be a pity to ruin what could be a good day.

SATURDAY 8th Those who know you well consider you to be highly creative and something of a visionary and this certainly appears to be backed up by the planets. Be sure that partners, employers and relatives are all aware of your extraordinary suggestions. Who knows, they might take you seriously. It looks as if you could be on to a real winner, but this does not mean you get the green light from the stars to take any kind of financial chance.

SUNDAY 9th Mercury is in beautiful aspect to Mars today, and will provide you with additional mental energy: you will possess the ability to study and put latent ideas and plans into dynamic action. Energetic and intellectual conditions are very favourable today for the realization of your dreams. Should you be owed money this would be a good time for enquiring when you can expect to be paid.

MONDAY 10th   Make an effort today to remind partners, loved ones and the family that they are forever in your thoughts, even when your attention is focused on the serious business of making a living. On this occasion, however, your true ambition is to be happy at home, even if it means cutting back on your responsibilities and commitments.

TUESDAY 11th   Today you can do much to further your worldly progress. Additional energy and enterprise are on your side, but you could also be rather extravagant. Take care that the more lively and enthusiastic side to your character is controlled or you could become impulsive and wreck the potential of this particular day.

WEDNESDAY 12th   Your birth sign tends to be associated with dreaming, but your present problems are far more down to earth. In fact, as the planets combine to put you to the test you have rarely been such a bundle of nerves. More importantly, if you fail today's challenge you will be handing over responsibility for your actions to those who, while possessing greater self-confidence, lack your sense of justice and fair play.

THURSDAY 13th   Venus in aspect to Saturn today seems to highlight a relationship with someone of a much greater age. It could be romantic, though not necessarily so. There may also be some financial stress, which could make you overly careful at a time when it will be more difficult than usual to express the way you feel. Never mind, you can leave this to another day.

FRIDAY 14th   The Sun in a beautiful aspect to Mercury will help you to put your point across to bosses or those in positions of authority, but don't for a moment think that the battle is over. In fact, powerful activity in your sign suggests that the real fight is yet to begin, and it may be some while yet before you demand the recognition you deserve.

SATURDAY 15th   The full Moon today in the sign of Libra suggests it would not be a good idea to fall foul of officialdom in any way, shape or form. Therefore, be scrupulous about drinking and driving and stick to all the rules of the road: risk-taking will only lead to problems which could turn out to be expensive, in one way or another. A good time, though, if you need to think through problems and come up with answers you can implement in a couple of days.

SUNDAY 16th   Whatever secrets you may have hanging over from the past, now is the time to tell others while they are in a mood to forgive and forget. Extremely potent planetary activity suggests there is a problem ahead which will have a long-lasting effect on your work. You will need the help and support of partners, friends and colleagues and this will not be difficult to obtain.

MONDAY 17th   Keep travel plans to a minimum today, even though others may be encouraging you to join them. Mercury's move into Taurus is a powerful factor that can for the most part be relied upon to work in your favour, but not while it forms a difficult aspect to the Moon today. Those closest to you will be in a determinedly stubborn mood and there is no point in attempting to shift them for the time being.

TUESDAY 18th   You are certainly in one of your active moods. However, today you may have a certain amount of difficulty keeping your temper in check, or possibly others are angry over joint arrangements or financial matters. Either way, don't forget that even if flying into a rage makes you feel better, it will achieve precious little. A friendly approach is likely to assist you far more and, besides, this evening is promising for romance so you don't want it to get off to a difficult start.

WEDNESDAY 19th   You will not need to do anything extraordinary to grab the attention of those around you today. On the other hand, with so much activity in your sign don't feel put out if friends or loved ones fail to live up to your high expectations. More than likely you are hoping for the impossible and need to be far more realistic at the moment.

THURSDAY 20th   If you are experiencing any kind of difficulty at home or at work, you could now be reaching a point when you believe you have finally cracked it. Unfortunately, because your ruling planet is about to go into retrograde movement, the chances are you will be deluding yourself. Avoid making any hasty decisions for the time being.

FRIDAY 21st   If you are the kind of Piscean who learns from your mistakes, you will know what can be achieved as far as creative and financial matters are concerned. Of course, with so much planetary activity in Aries, life will smile on you for some while yet. But remember that real wisdom cannot be discovered overnight and the planets have much to teach you yet.

SATURDAY 22nd   Venus is in a beautiful aspect to Pluto today and this should be a financially positive time; excellent too for investing in long-term insurance.

Your sex life assumes more importance than usual and many of you will be falling dramatically and seriously in love. However, do not make any hasty commitments.

SUNDAY 23rd Having tried, and possibly failed, with the softly-softly approach, you may be at a loss to know what to do next with long-running partnership or domestic disputes. To be candid, there is not a lot you can do: if others are still behaving in an unreasonable manner the best thing you can do is to take yourself out of the firing line. Let others chase after you for a while instead.

MONDAY 24th At the moment it is likely that you will be getting involved in details. You may even, for a change, thrive on them. In some ways, however, this could be negative: not least because you have an inclination to lose sight of your ultimate goal. Somewhere along the line today you will be given the chance to see things as a whole. Make certain you take it, even if it questions your overall direction.

TUESDAY 25th Although you are of a gentle and artistic temperament, there are times when you are constantly at war with yourself – and this certainly seems to be the case at this moment in time. The most likely battleground will be love and money. Indeed, you may even now be torn between the two. Somehow you must find room for both, and providing you maintain your confidence in your excellent judgement you will have no difficulty whatsoever.

WEDNESDAY 26th Outwardly you may be assertive and quiet, inwardly you are intensely romantic and inclined to extreme anxiety and despondency. It is essential today that you cultivate hope and stimulating companionship. Your greatest qualities are your sympathy for the underprivileged and your willingness to alleviate the suffering of other people.

THURSDAY 27th   Your life at the moment seems to be a matter of timing, but you must guard against dwelling too much in the past. Neptune, your planetary ruler, is now in Capricorn and may make it difficult for you to communicate with certain people who seem to be inhabiting a fantasy world. Financial success is assured if you make a determined effort to exploit your talents.

FRIDAY 28th   You are now forced to devote all your time to emotional ties because the planet suggests you can no longer afford to hedge your bets. However, there is a new Moon tomorrow and around this time you will realize that changes are unavoidable. It is simply a question of cutting out all the dead wood.

SATURDAY 29th   A new Moon today in the sign of Taurus gives you the opportunity to clear the decks and start again in all areas of life. It is likely, too, that you will be on the go more than usual as you have abundant energy and find it difficult to sit still for even a second. Romance which leaves the launching pad today will be positive and good.

SUNDAY 30th   Mercury is in beautiful aspect with Neptune and it will be easier for you to bridge gaps in many of your relationships. The whole day has a 'coming together' about it, and those of you with romance in mind should make sure you are out and about and that others are aware that you are available. Fresh relationships begun now will be important for some time to come.

MAY

MONDAY 1st   It is time you realized that you were put on this planet to play a special role in life. Too frequently you have failed to capitalize on your talents. Over the past couple of months or so you have confronted difficulties and restrictions with enormous bravery, and in the process have learnt to stand alone. New career opportunities now will provide you with the recognition and reward you so richly deserve.

TUESDAY 2nd   Today Mercury is in a beautiful aspect with Uranus and because of this whatever happens will be helpful in making plans for your career or leisure-time interests. Friendships (perhaps spiced with dynamic attraction) are likely to occur at this time. You may well be more attractive to others right now and it is up to you to make the most of this wonderful day.

WEDNESDAY 3rd   Mercury now moves into the sign of Gemini, which represents the home, property and family areas of life. Therefore, over the next few weeks or so you can expect minor changes to take place, some of which surprise you a good deal. It is likely, too, that relatives will be introducing you to new people who will quickly become firm friends. A great time for exchanging contracts and dealing with property matters in general.

THURSDAY 4th   There is a beautiful aspect between Venus and Jupiter today, and this is indicative of great happiness. Financial and social success is also likely. Your sensitivity is heightened and will be encouraging an appreciation of beauty. You will be doing everything you can to push ahead with your creative projects.

FRIDAY 5th   Throughout this day personal and partnership affairs are emphasized and in many respects situations will never be quite the same again. This is a time when you will begin to understand that one chapter or cycle of life must come to a close. The more adventurous, idealistic and progressive you are from now on, the greater your chance of personal and professional success.

SATURDAY 6th   Earlier in the year you were much preoccupied with financial arrangements, professional transactions and anything and everything connected with long-term security and comfort. Others have had enough time to make up their minds and keep their promises: now you must demand that they fulfil their obligations. This is also a day which heralds a totally new and decisive period in personal affairs.

SUNDAY 7th   You must stride ahead with added confidence. Emotionally, however, guard against impetuosity – although you are likely to fall head over heels in love with somebody, it will turn out to be only an infatuation. Furthermore, you must take a tougher line on joint financial arrangements and ensure that others are not being over-optimistic about the outcome of negotiations. Mentally you should be enjoying an exciting period and extracting the maximum from it.

MONDAY 8th   Allow Aries to be the initiator and pioneer, Taurus the builder, and so on. Your reputation as a poet is apt, well earned and deserved. Channel your energy towards increasing your prestige, personally and professionally. You will then accomplish all the goals you have set yourself and a feeling of wellbeing and satisfaction should be your reward.

TUESDAY 9th   Today you should try hard to keep your emotions under control. No matter what you have been told or recently discovered, do not force others to state their intentions. The new Moon on the 29th will alter so much, both personally and financially, that it will seem as if you are being asked to choose between an established way of life and a complete change of direction.

WEDNESDAY 10th   It is a time for new resolutions and promises, and the first must be to never again become so compromised over money and joint arrangements. Make the next few days a time for recovery, both emotionally and in other directions, too.

THURSDAY 11th   This is a time for digging deep within yourself and not being afraid to make a big break. There is a difficult full Moon on the 14th so you can expect the odd emotional skirmish. Despite this you will be optimistic. Many unexpected doors are going to be opened to you and the further you are ready to travel, the greater your success.

FRIDAY 12th   Mercury is in beautiful aspect with Jupiter today and because of this you will find that other people are only too willing to cooperate with you. Furthermore, their mood will be buoyant, optimistic and positive and no matter how you begin the day this will prove to be contagious. This evening could be flirty and fun, but do not take yourself too seriously.

SATURDAY 13th   The stars suggest that you will not be playing the supporting role for very much longer. Soon you will be striking out and expecting more attention and recognition. Many of you seem to prefer challenges, and if you have a special relationship with somebody born under the sign of Gemini or Virgo you now know that shortly you will have to find a new overall format for the future.

SUNDAY 14th This is full Moon day and you will need to fight to maintain peace: those closest to you are likely to be emotionally charged and it is important that you persuade them to make some kind of change. On a social level, something may not come up to your high expectations, so try to be a little bit more realistic.

MONDAY 15th You are renowned for your breadth of vision and high standing, both the result of experience. Your mission in life now is it profit from all you have suffered. This is one of the most decisive periods you have known for partnership affairs, and all concerned should finally come to their senses.

TUESDAY 16th The Sun is in a beautiful aspect to your ruling planet, Neptune, and this will give you not only complete confidence but also inspiration. It will certainly help if you are artistic. However, with Neptune activated in this way your ideas must be channelled positively in order to avoid escapism or confusion.

WEDNESDAY 17th Planetary activity today is giving you the urge to crash through barriers and live according to your own rules. Like fish, you want to swim freely without impediment. Others may not fully understand your motives and conflict could arise because they feel a little let down. Cash may recently have been a problem, but you now feel you have learnt to juggle your resources successfully.

THURSDAY 18th Today Venus moves into the sign of Taurus and this will certainly be helping you if you are creative. It is also good for casual romance, but it is imperative you do not take it seriously for the time being. Enjoy your freedom while you have it. A brother or sister may have some interesting advice and may be of use to you in some way.

FRIDAY 19th There is no need to play safe now or worry about the impression you are having on other people. Aspects today give a clear indication that you will go from strength to strength and in the process find greater emotional security and awareness. You are starting a constructive period.

SATURDAY 20th You may have valid reasons for spending time away from your usual haunts. You seem to be chasing round trying to make contact for professional reasons. However, do not allow other people to stop you from broadening your horizons. Out of the blue you will be given a chance to prove yourself successful.

SUNDAY 21st A wonderful aspect between the Sun and Uranus adds an exciting but intense feel to the day. Many of you will experience unexpected financial gains and all Pisceans will certainly benefit from increased dynamism and outgoing interests. There are likely to be long-term changes in both your career and inner life.

MONDAY 22nd Today the Sun moves into the sign of Gemini and you begin a period when most of the emphasis will be on property, family and relatives. Never mind, even you need rest on occasions and you should use this period to study at home or make changes to your daily routine. You will find those with whom you live far more cooperative than usual.

TUESDAY 23rd The Moon is in your sign and the true spirit of Pisces should shine through now. That part of your chart related to travel and inspiration should enable you to theorize to your heart's content without being thought of as 'too clever by half'. You may well decide to make a change that has been on your mind for most of this year.

WEDNESDAY 24th   Today Mercury moves into retrograde movement: you are therefore advised to double-check arrangements if it is necessary for you to travel over the next few weeks or so. There is nothing to fear but muddle with documents or paperwork could lead to a certain amount of aggravation. Avoid litigation and making unnecessary changes until this planet resumes direct movement.

THURSDAY 25th   It is likely that you have been caught in the cross-fire recently. Warring factions had better sort out their views or you may well turn on them with ammunition they never knew you possessed. The full Moon that took place on the 14th was your signal to stop playing safe.

FRIDAY 26th   Mars moves into your opposite sign of Virgo today and this will certainly be enlivening all your relationships. On the positive side, you will find those closest to you more physical and sexy. But on the negative, they will be ready to do battle on the slightest pretext. You will need your undoubted Piscean charm if you are to keep the peace during this period.

SATURDAY 27th   Mars lines up with Uranus today and cashwise you could be gaining quite unexpectedly, or perhaps through unusual people. Do not hesitate to take on board fresh ideas or even switch direction where money is concerned. Romantically, too, it is a time for attempting the untried and being as experimental as possible. However, do not play with the feelings of other people.

SUNDAY 28th For some reason you appear to be holding on to the past with determination, and no one can understand your motives or even your dilemma. Maybe you are disappointed and disillusioned by the recent behaviour of loved ones or colleagues, but surely you know better than most that they should be pitied rather than blamed.

MONDAY 29th This is new Moon day and it occurs in the sign of Gemini. This will do much to alter your life both financially and on a personal level. It is also possible that this will be a time of choices and change of direction. News which comes in from the family or in connection with property is likely to hearten you, and there seems to be reason for a minor celebration.

TUESDAY 30th This is a good day for surprising those around you with your inventiveness, creativity and dedication. Emotionally and personally you are something of a mystery, and often a headache to those who know and love you best. However, with Neptune in Capricorn you must now be more selective in your choice of friends or you could experience disillusionment and deception.

WEDNESDAY 31st Past disappointments and battles have certainly taught you a harsh lesson, but no one is likely to get the better of you at the moment as you are drawing on these experiences. You now seem to have set your heart on achieving something more than material wealth and security.

JUNE

THURSDAY 1st Certain emotional attachments or family ties seem to be making you feel guilty or uncomfortable because of your decision to change direction or simply take off. But you have given a lot of time and thought to your plans and it would be a pity to miss out on what could be the chance of a lifetime.

FRIDAY 2nd You are now given an opportunity to prove what you mean by freedom and independence. Planetary activity highlights travel and connections abroad and it will be a long time before you are again in such a strong position to control your own destiny.

SATURDAY 3rd This is certainly likely to be a hectic and enlightening time, especially where work is concerned. In many respects you seem to be spoilt for choice, and you ought to spend some time away from your usual environment in order to look over the whole picture – and as soon as possible.

SUNDAY 4th Try to show some self-control and discipline so that you can enjoy life to the full. In the past you have suffered dearly for indiscretion, either in your personal relationships or over money. Now you can and will be able to plan your future with greater confidence.

MONDAY 5th There is a truly beautiful aspect between the Sun and Mercury and this is likely to affect the personal side to life. Planets are giving you the perfect chance to forget about all the emotional dramas of the past and bounce back with a vengeance.

TUESDAY 6th The Moon in your opposite sign of Virgo gives you a new dimension and the confidence to say 'no' to those who are encouraging you to join them in a plan or project you basically mistrust. After months of agonizing you can finally decide on where you will be happiest.

WEDNESDAY 7th Your instincts should tell you that you are about to make a major breakthrough where work matters are concerned – or a new occupation even. In any event, with Pluto in your angle of long-distance travel this is a time for golden opportunities which you should not let slip through your fingers.

THURSDAY 8th Partners and loved ones must be given a sympathetic ear even though you are still preoccupied with money. Put family matters first and force others to face up to things they have been trying to avoid. Conflicts over money matters and joint finances must not be allowed to make you feel insecure. This evening it is likely that you will be concentrating on matters of the heart.

FRIDAY 9th Uranus is now in retrograde movement. This suggests that over the next few weeks or so you must double-check all your arrangements with friends, contacts and acquaintances as muddles are expected in these areas. A little bit of forethought will save you a great deal of trouble.

SATURDAY 10th The stars seem to signify the beginning of a new phase in your life: make the most of it and dispose of anything that is outdated. They are also giving you an opportunity to settle a family or domestic dispute. Do whatever is necessary to make peace; after all, as a Pisces you are not hampered with a hyper-sensitive ego.

SUNDAY 11th Today Venus moves into the sign of Gemini, which will be casting a rosy and contented glow over domestic affairs, the family and property matters. From here on you will be inclined to take your pleasures on your own base, and will be acting the role of host/hostess in the most charming and successful way.

MONDAY 12th Make the most of any time spent by yourself today: what you discover during contemplation will be extremely useful in the future. In general this is a time to evaluate what has taken place recently. There have been many changes and not all of them to your liking. Ask what needs to be changed now in order to make tomorrow more exciting.

TUESDAY 13th The full Moon today at the zenith of your chart suggests that matters which have been hidden are finally coming to light and this will go a long way to put your mind at ease. It is a wonderful time for making plans, both professionally and otherwise, although not a time for leaping into action.

WEDNESDAY 14th Because of your active imagination you sometimes find it difficult to keep pace with your own ideas. Right now, the stars seem to suggest that you will have the opportunity to realize a dream. However, the more you attempt, the less you will achieve, so try to streamline your activities and concentrate on your most inventive ideas.

THURSDAY 15th Pisces is the sign of the visionary, and now you have a chance to be a pioneer as well.

The stars will be giving you an opportunity to put some of your more choice ideas into practice. How successful you are will depend on finding the right balance between reality and theory. It is one thing to know what needs to be done, quite another to find the right way of doing it.

FRIDAY 16th There may be a strong temptation to spend your way out of trouble, and this, of course, will not work. What is needed now is not a fresh injection of cash but a new approach to both professional and personal problems. You might even need to shut yourself away from outside influences for a while and think again about the best way forward.

SATURDAY 17th Mercury now resumes direct movement and any differences between yourself and those closest to you begin to evaporate. It is a time when you can seriously consider signing on the dotted line, chasing work or making plans to travel in the very near future. Those whom you believe to be your rivals seem to have less power to disrupt your life and ambitions.

SUNDAY 18th Mercury is in a beautiful aspect with Venus today; therefore, wherever you go you will be greeted by cooperative, smiling faces, and it should not be difficult to find romance. Make this a fun day, one when you please yourself rather than going out of your way in typical Pisces style to please other people. You cannot always think of others: this is a time for keeping a high profile and getting your own way.

MONDAY 19th The Moon in your sign will help you to feel more confident about the future. Don't be afraid to push ahead with plans or schemes that have been under consideration for far too long. However, remember to keep loved ones and colleagues in the picture where your movements and motives are concerned if you want to avoid serious disagreement. You cannot afford to antagonize or anger the wrong people right now.

TUESDAY 20th Today you should be able to find the perfect compromise between career and financial matters. Life may not have been too easy recently, but your determination has not gone unnoticed by those who matter most. In fact, your efforts over this period are about to be paid in full – and probably with interest.

WEDNESDAY 21st What occurs today could come as something of a surprise and as a result you may find you neglect to take advantage of the situation. Whatever chances you are offered don't think for a moment you have not earned them or do not deserve the chance to shine. Use them, profit by them and, above all, enjoy them.

THURSDAY 22nd Today the Sun moves into the sign of Cancer, which represents creative, pleasure-loving, romantic and speculative areas of life. Over the next few weeks you should cram in as much socializing as possible in order to take advantage of this placing. If you are creative you can certainly push ahead and present your ideas to other people in the knowledge that they are going to be well received.

FRIDAY 23rd Your short-term prospects seem to be getting rosier by the day, but long-term difficulties will continue for a while. As a Piscean you possess many talents, but your ability to over-dramatize is almost an art form. Regrettably you cannot push to one side what is worrying you – it keeps nagging away at the back of your mind. You will just have to confront those who have upset you, even at the risk of creating a scene.

SATURDAY 24th No doubt you are only too aware of the fact that life has been quite difficult. This is because Saturn has been wending its way through your sign and has on occasions kept you very much tied to the past. Now the planets are making you feel that all you have endured has been worth while. In fact, very soon you will realize that the future is already looking very much brighter.

SUNDAY 25th Today try to concentrate on what you do best. There are times when you become overwhelmed by a crazy desire to do something rash and this would be completely wrong at the moment. Right now pride and money are at stake and you could very well regret hasty decisions therefore.

MONDAY 26th No matter what cards you have been dealt recently, you are now in a position to play them for all they are worth. If urgent action is needed where cash or business matters are concerned, don't be afraid to take it. Praise and recognition isn't enough and you must insist on being paid your true value which is a great deal.

TUESDAY 27th Saturn is in a beautiful aspect with Neptune today. Ideas are likely to take constructive shape, and any inspiration should be seriously considered. Furthermore, you are in a rational and logical mood for a change, and when others approach you with their ideas and suggestions you will be able to sort the useful from the worthless. Your concentration is intense today and you should use it to clear up the backlog of work which has been around for a considerable time.

WEDNESDAY 28th　Today a beautiful new Moon is shining in the sign of Cancer. This will help to liven up your romantic life, and if you are fancy-free for Heaven's sake get out and about and circulate. A good time, too, for presenting new creative and artistic ideas to other people. Those of you with children will find them better behaved and more cooperative than they have been for a while.

THURSDAY 29th　This is an excellent day for making plans for the future. Try to tie up loose ends and ensure that plans for the rest of the year are both realistic and wide ranging. You couldn't wish for a more productive time for finding jobs and setting new goals. If you can dream about it then you can also do it. All you have to do is believe. Any chance to socialize this evening should be snapped up – you need to let off steam.

FRIDAY 30th　Uranus is in aspect with Pluto today, suggesting a period which is likely to be filled with turbulence and new beginnings in which you may not have any say. But luckily, as a Piscean you possess a great fund of flexibility – which you are certainly going to need during the day ahead. Ideas that pop into your head should be noted and saved for the future.

JULY

SATURDAY 1st　Saturn is in aspect with your ruling planet, Neptune, today and this will help you to clear the clutter from your mind and see exactly what is important. Having done this, lay down a few plans and prepare to work slowly towards the realization of your dreams. With steady application you are capable of accomplishing a great deal today.

SUNDAY 2nd Remember that whatever decisions you make today you will need to live with for some time. Therefore, if you are in any doubt at all wait until the new Moon on the 27th. It is likely that this evening you will discover where, why and when you have been deceived. In this instance even your imagination will be baffled by the facts.

MONDAY 3rd The Moon in your opposite sign of Virgo is certainly stirring up your personal relationships today. In fact, other people could be springing a few surprises. Never mind, their ingenuity and imagination will astound even you. Romantically, a time for getting out and meeting fresh faces. Romance isn't serious, but it could be a good deal of fun.

TUESDAY 4th The Moon continues in Virgo, creating restlessness and insecurity. But rest assured that your current feelings are caused by an over active imagination – once you realize this you will be more in control. Wait a while before making decisions as it is unlikely that you have all the facts at your fingertips at this moment in time.

WEDNESDAY 5th Today Venus enters the sign of Cancer, which will be heralding a certain amount of 'good times'. If you are single you will be reluctant to become seriously involved with the opposite sex, preferring to enjoy a multitude of faces rather than making a commitment to one. There is a rosy glow over artistic matters and everything connected with offspring.

THURSDAY 6th Saturn moves into retrograde movement today. This suggests that you should not rely on any promises or commitments made by friends, acquaintances and contacts. They no doubt mean well but circumstances beyond their control may prevent them fulfilling their obligation – be independent.

FRIDAY 7th No matter how many times you have tried a particular avenue for your talents and received a negative response, now is the time to take that same route once more. This time you are likely to be successful. Furthermore, in order to get the right answers it is important to ask the right questions. The time is certainly propitious for looking after your own needs for a change.

SATURDAY 8th The aspect between Uranus and Pluto could lead to exciting conditions, particularly on the work front. However, if you are creative, you may feel that you are suffering from the proverbial 'mental block'. If so, turn your attention elsewhere rather than wallowing in a lather of indecision and frustration. Failure to heed this advice could find you wasting this entire period when you could at least be making progress in other directions.

SUNDAY 9th Basically, you have been consumed with the idea of making changes in either your professional or personal life, or perhaps both. If you believe that the time has come to grow or expand your horizons, then permit nothing to stand in your way. However, with mighty Saturn still active in your Sun sign, you must be absolutely clear about what you are trying to achieve. If not, your destination may be no better than your starting point.

MONDAY 10th Sexy, aggressive and enterprising Mars is in wonderful aspect to your ruling planet, Neptune. Right now, then, you are more confident than you have been for quite some time, and ready to move under your own steam instead of continually waiting for other people to motivate you. You are more magnetic, too, and this could prove irresistible to the opposite sex. Lots to look forward to.

TUESDAY 11th Mercury moves into the sign of Cancer today and from here on it is likely you will be attracted to new leisure-time activities of a mental rather than purely physical nature. For example, you could develop a fascination for chess or backgammon. If you have children, there seems to be a great deal of increased activity on their behalf.

WEDNESDAY 12th The full Moon today occurs in the sign of Capricorn, the friendship area of your chart, and it is possible a contact or someone you trust will let you down. Before you fly into a rage a little double-checking might show that they had little hope of fulfilling their duties to you due to changing circumstances.

THURSDAY 13th The planets today signify that your priority right now must be to strike a balance between financial and emotional needs. Above all, don't allow other people's behaviour or problems to undermine you. In fact, take note of what is occurring now because these themes are likely to return later in the year. Remember that no life is so difficult that it can't be made easier by the way you lead it.

FRIDAY 14th Tensions which have been simmering beneath the surface for quite some time are now ready to burst into the open. At least one important personal relationship may never be quite the same again. However, you must try to remember, however painful, that life is about change, good and bad. Once you recognize this you will be more accepting. Luckily the stars herald a change of scene as well as emphasis, and this will go a long way to cheering you up.

SATURDAY 15th Pisceans loathe discipline imposed upon them by other people. Nevertheless, you are capable of great sacrifices if you have a particular objective in mind. There is hardly likely to be a better time for getting a long-treasured scheme or project off the drawing board and into action: the Sun in Cancer certainly seems to be firing you with enthusiasm and setting you on your way.

SUNDAY 16th The Moon is in your sign today and you would do well to remember that successful undertakings are accomplished by keeping long-term objectives in mind while concentrating on the job in hand. There will be some set-backs over the next few days, but it will then be clear that you are heading in precisely the right direction as far as property, family and cash matters are concerned. In fact, your confidence and determination should be soaring.

MONDAY 17th Mars and Pluto are in aspect today. As these two planets are related through rulership in the sign of Scorpio, their influences are somewhat balanced. But the contribution of increased energy from Mars and the blocking influence of Pluto could cause difficulties which can only be overcome by sheer force. There may be a sudden ruthless striving for power, but the stars are certainly helping to push you up the ladder of success, even at the price of unpopularity.

TUESDAY 18th   Although you would never intentionally say anything to hurt another person, neither are you the type to hold back when you believe by speaking you can do some good. However, there may have been times recently when you have said more than was needed or wise. Your words will return to haunt you today, and where necessary you will need to make apologies or amends: an error acknowledged is a battle won.

WEDNESDAY 19th   Mars is in beautiful aspect with Uranus and this is likely to be an eventful day, a time for the unexpected and, perhaps, the exciting. Confidences are likely to be long-lasting. However, care is necessary when making new friends and acquaintances: their influence may not be all it seems. An extremely interesting time, and one when you will be full of enterprise, originality and insight. Your personal magnetism should make for an interesting love life.

THURSDAY 20th   The Sun in aspect with Pluto today provides you with an eventful time, although the benefits may be derived at a later date. There is a strong emphasis on cash and the possibility of beginning a new phase – perhaps a complete change of direction, though not without certain difficulties.

FRIDAY 21st   One of the rules of the planets states that what you gain from life is in direct proportion to what you put in. Therefore, don't think twice about accepting what is on offer today, even if you believe others deserve it more than you, which is probably the case. Half of the problem is that you are far too modest and this constantly holds you back: the less talented people around then make off with all the glory that should be yours. Expect the best for yourself right now and you will get it.

SATURDAY 22nd The Moon in Taurus today will certainly be gingering you up on a physical level: you seem unable to sit still for longer than a few seconds. Because of this there will be increased contact with neighbours, friends and anybody who is close by. Romance is likely to be of the 'brief encounter' variety and must not be taken too seriously. Good ideas also abound and it might be an idea to write them down before you forget – you know how absent-minded you can be on occasions.

SUNDAY 23rd Today the Sun enters the sign of Leo, the area of life devoted to your ability to serve and aid other people, which, of course, as a Piscean is quite considerable. Therefore, during the ensuing weeks it is likely that on more than one occasion you will be playing 'the good samaritan'. On the work front there is likely to be a more positive and optimistic feel, which will indirectly rub off on you.

MONDAY 24th The Moon in the area of your chart devoted to family, property and relatives seems to suggest that it is an ideal time for making small adjustments or changes where these matters are concerned. There may also be some exciting news in connection with an engagement, birth or marriage. Certainly the family will keep you run off your feet and it is unlikely that you will have a chance to escape this evening. Because of this, the single fish can wave goodbye to chances of romance. Never mind, there is always another day.

TUESDAY 25th The Moon today moves into the sign of Cancer, the area of life devoted to creativity, children, sports, romance and pleasure – in fact everything you enjoy most. On a romantic level you are flirty but not serious, and must take care not to make promises or commitments you have no intention of keeping. This is also an ideal time for being honest with a member of the opposite sex if you are feeling that you would prefer to maintain a friendship rather than get into anything more intense.

WEDNESDAY 26th Mercury moves into Leo today and there could be rumours of a contract, or the possibility of a professional trip. Members of staff or people you meet during your everyday working life will be strongly affected by your Piscean charm and you will be making new friends from the contacts. An ideal time for meetings and signing on the dotted line.

THURSDAY 27th Clear the clutter from your brain and the dead wood from your life in order to make your progress a good deal smoother. Furthermore, a beautiful aspect between Venus and Pluto today suggests financial prosperity. Your sex life is likely to assume more importance; and many of you may be carried away by a mad infatuation – which fortunately you will not take too seriously.

FRIDAY 28th The Sun is in beautiful aspect with Mercury today and because of this, no matter where you go, you will find that other people are confident, warm, generous and optimistic. Therefore, if you have been biding your time and waiting for the opportunity to do someone a favour or do a certain job, now is the time to leap into action. On a personal level you are likely to be drawing closer to that special someone in your life. There is much to look forward to.

SATURDAY 29th The Sun is in a beautiful aspect to Jupiter and it is just the time to lay down important plans for your professional life. If you happen to be at work you may learn of some exciting news, or you could become romantically involved with a workmate. Lady Luck is riding along with you right now and you must push ahead with everything dearest to your heart.

SUNDAY 30th Venus enters the sign of Leo today and from here on it is likely that when it comes to socializing you will be mixing business with pleasure far more than usual. It could be that ulterior motives are at work here, and if so you are likely to be successful. Some of you may become romantically involved with those you meet professionally.

MONDAY 31st The Moon in your opposite sign of Virgo suggests that those close to you will be changeable, and perhaps unreliable. Because of this it is an ideal time for maintaining your independence rather than expecting others to gallop in like the cavalry and rescue you from a potentially dangerous situation.

AUGUST

TUESDAY 1st Mars is in aspect with Jupiter today and because of this you can do a great deal to further your worldly ambitions. You will possess additional energy and enterprise, which will no doubt help you to champion your cause. However, an inclination to be wasteful and over-extravagant will need to be controlled. Apart from this, the day seems to be lively and enthusiastic, although you may also experience certain difficulties with the impulsive side to your nature.

WEDNESDAY 2nd Today Jupiter finally resumes direct movement and complications in your personal life could finally disappear. If you have felt that you are taking one step forward and three steps back where financial matters are concerned, you can now be assured that this is a thing of the past. Be prepared to present your wonderful ideas to other people: they will be prepared to listen and act upon them.

THURSDAY 3rd There is a beautiful aspect between Venus and Jupiter today and it is certainly likely to be positive and a time when finances could improve. Life will be much more enjoyable and you will be showing increased generosity and sympathy. However, if you are currently on a diet you may have great difficulty in avoiding rich food. Always remember, though, that you are the master of your own fate and cannot be battered around by anybody else, and that includes the stars. Your destiny is in your own hands.

FRIDAY 4th The Moon in the water sign of Scorpio suggests that there is an element of fresh experience in the air. A very harmonious period seems to be starting today and you will be making your mark on a close relationship or love affair. Work matters and established business ties are also under lucky influences, although something that has been simmering away in the background could erupt quite unexpectedly.

SATURDAY 5th For some time now you may have been considering making substantial property investments, but with so many important and far-reaching changes taking place, time has been at a premium and even the preliminary step has not yet been taken. Right now the stars are helping to illuminate the way forward. But even so, don't be in too much of a rush – you have investments elsewhere and are urged to consolidate your financial position rather than over-extend yourself.

SUNDAY 6th   Career and finances could be a lot better, but there are plenty of compensations in the form of a satisfying love life and the much needed support of close friends. There are also likely to be major implications concerning long-term arrangements. If you can examine your life and sort out what is of value and what is not, it will be both enlightening and liberating.

MONDAY 7th   It is important that you be cautious and make decisions based on thorough and practical assessments of any situation, always taking into account any and every eventuality. Having done this you should be able to proceed in leaps and bounds. But if you want your life to change for the better you must be prepared to take a calculated risk.

TUESDAY 8th   Today Pluto resumes direct movement; therefore, if you have experienced complications with higher education, foreign affairs or long-distance travel you can be assured that these are now over and you can push ahead in these areas. This is also a good time for making major changes in life, always assuming you have done the ground work first.

WEDNESDAY 9th   Mercury will be moving to your opposite sign of Virgo and introducing a theme of change into all your closest relationships, both on a professional and personal level. Those of you in steady relationships may be tempted into extra curricula fun and you are advised, particularly if you are male, to keep this tendency under strict control. A good time, too, for forming professional partnerships.

THURSDAY 10th   Today is the full Moon and it is likely that in one of your personal relationships feelings that have been simmering under the surface will finally explode and provide you with a few heart-stopping moments. It seems you are totally unaware how deeply and passionately somebody was feeling about a decision or a project; now you must be more considerate of their hopes and wishes.

FRIDAY 11th There may be a tendency for you to become occupied and entrenched in some kind of disagreement, and because of this it will be impossible to get a true perspective and see life in a wider context. Being a worrier, the chances are you have already analysed the situation to the point where it doesn't seem to make sense any more. On the work front you are at a delicate stage as far as negotiations are concerned, but for the best results postpone a final decision until the new Moon on the 26th – if you can wait that long.

SATURDAY 12th With Venus and the Sun squatting in the area of your chart devoted to pleasure, fun and romance, it will be a rare fish who ends this period without some significant event of a romantic or partnership nature. An upheaval or change of residence could be about to take place, but make sure all negotiations are finalized before this month is out.

SUNDAY 13th There is an unpredictable quality about the day due to the presence of the Moon in your sign, and if you have been hoping for things to go strictly according to plan you may have to do some quick rethinking. However, there seems to be much ahead of you that is good and it will be a complete waste of time to worry about what might have been. Concentrate on the present and what is, because success is almost within your reach.

MONDAY 14th A cluster of planets in your opposite sign of Virgo indicates that you are not yet out of the woods as far as a delicate professional issue is concerned. The situation seems to be a little threatening because you feel out of your depth. But you have more power to influence the outcome than you realize. If you can recognize this and act appropriately, you will subsequently be able to set a positive course of action into motion. Deadlocks may occur in your love life but you should try to talk through problems – and keep on talking till your mate listens.

TUESDAY 15th People you least expect to help you could reappear, and with their assistance you should find you fall on your feet and are able to make an important decision which involves a small risk. The stars are highly inspiring for creative and imaginative work, and where your personal life is concerned you can be confident that one particular relationship is definitely on.

WEDNESDAY 16th After the trials and tribulations over Saturn in recent months, today will mark the conclusion of many of the difficulties and frustrations this planet may have wrought. It looks as if you are about to launch all manner of new beginnings, and they are under brilliant stars. The most likely outcome is a thorough overhaul and re-evaluation of your life style and the introduction of much-needed changes or reforms.

THURSDAY 17th Mars in Libra will be increasing your energy levels and motivation in a positive way. However, you may find it difficult to slow down and pay attention to important details. You will possibly be starting a new phase where financial and professional matters are concerned, and with your Piscean intelligence and perception will be able to make the most of it. You will, of course, always show concern for those who are out on a limb, but don't neglect personal matters which need a great deal of tidying up.

FRIDAY 18th   A long-standing disagreement must be settled if you are to protect your long-term financial security: it may be a case of coming to your senses and not allowing emotions to influence your judgement. Fortunately you have wise and sympathetic allies who realize that, business wise, this is a most decisive and important phase and you now need a good deal of support if you are to triumph.

SATURDAY 19th   The Moon in Gemini suggests that you will be receiving a lot of news and advice from loved ones, including relatives. You should listen to what they have to say and be prepared to act upon their words because this is an extremely good time for implementing a strategic and carefully-planned move. Plenty of activity this evening, although it may all come as a bit of a surprise.

SUNDAY 20th   Venus is in a beautiful aspect to the Sun and your day will be full of harmony, colour, socializing and, above all else, romance. It is possible, too, that somebody you had forgotten about may be getting in touch, and this certainly makes your day. However, avoid spending money unnecessarily, especially if you are hoping to impress someone it – simply won't work.

MONDAY 21st   It is likely that you will now be benefiting from the wisdom gained through past problems. Events which begin today will show quite clearly that one particular ambition you have is fruitless. This may be financial, professional or career related. If you can let go and modify your plan, it should produce the results you hoped for.

TUESDAY 22nd The stars will be offering you the opportunity to strengthen a romantic attachment or cement a family tie. This does not mean that you will not be out and about this evening, because activity certainly seems too be emphasized. However, do not take yourself to seriously if you are single: you may fool yourself into believing that you have met 'the right person'. Be prepared to wait and see how the situation develops.

WEDNESDAY 23rd Today Venus moves into your opposite sign of Virgo, throwing a harmonious glow over all your existing relationships. Many of you may decide to make a commitment such as an engagement, or even a marriage. Should you be fancy-free, during the next month or so you will have the chance to meet many fascinating and attrative members of the opposite sex. Don't let the grass grow under your feet.

THURSDAY 24th The Sun moves into your opposite sign of Virgo, and this suggests that you are beginning a month when it will pay you to cooperate as much as possible with other people. Independent plans could go awry, but those who are prepared to work in harness with others can make good progress during this period.

FRIDAY 25th Today Mercury lines up with your ruling planet Neptune and this suggests a coming together of some description. It may be that you are forming a professional partnership, or perhaps falling in love. Either way this promises to be a productive and lucky period. If you are already in a steady relationship, past differences can be dealt with in record time and you will be back on the road to greater understanding.

SATURDAY 26th The new Moon in your opposite sign of Virgo will be bringing into your life new people and faces. Situations will be changing in existing relationships, too, though they are likely to be good and positive and nothing for you to become nervous or worried about. You have plenty to look forward to at the moment.

SUNDAY 27th Today there is a beautiful aspect between Mercury and Uranus and you may find yourself suddenly attracted to those who would not normally appeal to you. People around you have ingenious ideas and if you are prepared to work alongside them this could lead to greater prosperity in the future.

MONDAY 28th You certainly seem to have learnt to take set-backs in your stride, and though work colleagues will be taxing your patience to the limit, the best course of action is to say little and wait a while before taking appropriate action. Give them enough rope and they will tie themselves in knots.

TUESDAY 29th The aspects today suggest that you may be seriously considering independent moves and going it alone on one particular career proposition. If you do take this decision, make a thorough and objective initial assessment of all the facts. After all, you don't want any nasty surprises at a later date, do you?

WEDNESDAY 30th You seem to be coming to your senses as far as an emotional relationship is concerned and you can now tie up a number of loose ends and say goodbye to certain people without a trace of guilt or remorse. This will leave you free to concentrate on people who have your best interests at heart.

THURSDAY 31st A confrontation with a loved one or colleague may be necessary at this moment in time in order to put your point of view across. A more forceful and self-interested approach on your part will be necessary because, let's face it, as a Piscean you prefer to allow other people to take the initiative. Now is the time for stepping out of character and producing a few surprised faces around you. A good time, too, for those of you connected with foreign affairs.

SEPTEMBER

FRIDAY 1st Today you are likely to be at your most outgoing, living up to your reputation as a smooth talker. Luckily, because Saturn is in touch with your ruling planet Neptune, any promises you give are likely to be fulfilled at a later date. In your personal life you will be demanding unswerving loyalty from those closest to you, but you should now be reorganizing your life and perhaps searching for greater security and responsibility in a new environment.

SATURDAY 2nd The Moon at the zenith of your chart makes this an ideal time for making plans of a professional nature. There is likely to be a feeling of change at your place of employment, although there is nothing for you to fear. People you meet whilst going about your daily duties should be cultivated as they may help you to get a project off the launching pad.

SUNDAY 3rd Mercury is in a beautiful aspect with Jupiter today; therefore, no matter where you are travelling you will be meeting bright, sunny, optimistic people and their mood cannot but help rub off on you in some way. If you have someone special you will be contributing a great deal to their quality of life with your sense of humour, warmth and kindness.

MONDAY 4th With the Moon in Capricorn there seems to be a considerable amount of change and movement in the friends and acquaintance area of life. If you are the kind of Piscean whose job relies on contacts, do not hesitate to get in touch as they should be able to put a 'good thing your way'. This evening is an ideal time for visits to clubs, and in this way you may find romance.

TUESDAY 5th It is likely that you will acquire a new ambition during the course of today. Something someone says sets off that creative and inspired imagination of yours, but you must make sure that it does not remain a pipe-dream. And the only way to do this is to follow through to the bitter end. Socially, this evening an unexpected invitation may delight you and although you may not feel like going out persuade yourself to do so.

WEDNESDAY 6th The Moon today is in the sign of Aquarius, putting you in a contemplative and intuitive mood for the next couple of days. Much good work can be done in the background of things and if you are involved in research you can expect a progressive time. You will be sensing vibrations and atmospheres between people you may be visiting.

THURSDAY 7th Today Mars begins to travel through the watery sign of Scorpio. You will be highly motivated, with tremendous amounts of energy, and are set to achieve great things. Your vitality, zest and initiative will help to emphasize successful themes. However, there are sure to be some arguments or resistance from work and you will need to placate and reassure them.

FRIDAY 8th   Passionate Mars is in the sensitive area of your chart, as are stimulating companions, excitement and even a new love affair. Your homing instincts could be strong and this may be an ideal time for putting a relationship on a more secure footing.

SATURDAY 9th   Today the full Moon occurs in your sign and it will pay you to keep a low profile. Should you present ideas to people it may be without doing the necessary research and homework and you could make a fool of yourself. This can easily be avoided if you remember that full Moons should be used for making plans, but not for leaping into action.

SUNDAY 10th   Venus is in a beautiful aspect to your ruling planet Neptune, and you are looking good, feeling good and ready to tackle the world full on. Any creative work you are involved with will certainly be well received and successful. Romance is in the air this evening. Make sure you are out and about ready to take advantage of the fact.

MONDAY 11th   You may be tempted to take on more responsibilities, especially if financial gains are at stake. Try to be satisfied with existing achievements and resist the temptation to continually strive for more. With the Moon in the cash area of life, fluctuations are a distinct possibility, so play it safe.

TUESDAY 12th   No one would dream of denying that you have been successful recently, but now is the time to rest, unwind and spend more time with loved ones. A new phase will be starting in your professional life soon, but in the meantime it is an ideal time to take a break. Alternatively, it could prove successful if you are considering buying or selling property.

WEDNESDAY 13th   Venus is in a beautiful aspect to Uranus today and may be marked by a memorable social occasion and an improvement in all round conditions. Furthermore, there is the possibility of an unexpected dynamic relationship, or the termination of one, although the former seems more likely. A sudden general influence from others is likely, and the unexpected will centre in your love life.

THURSDAY 14th   Venus lines up with Pluto today and this should be financially positive. For example, it will be an excellent time to consider safe investments or long-term insurance. Your sex life is likely to be more important than usual and many of you may fall suddenly and dramatically in love.

FRIDAY 15th   The Sun today is in a wonderful aspect with your ruling planet Neptune. This should certainly be helpful if you are artistic, although you will need to channel your inspiration in a positive way. It is likely, too, that you will be able to push ahead with a relationship, mainly due to your own confidence, warmth and generosity. Many of you may be making commitments at this period.

SATURDAY 16th   Venus today moves into the sign of Libra, and because of this there is a certain amount of harmony and good luck in connection with business, officialdom and bureaucracy. Therefore, if you have been haunted by problems in these areas you can think positively and believe that your wonderful Piscean charm cannot fail to win over any opposition.

SUNDAY 17th The Moon today has moved into the sign of Cancer and will be introducing a light-hearted influence into matters related to children, arts, creativity and the social side to life. Many invitations will be pouring in during the next few days and you must be selective and go where you will find the warmest welcome.

MONDAY 18th The Moon in Cancer will bode well for those of you who are dealing with children, teachers or parents. If you are concerned about the welfare of a younger person your mind will be put at ease at this moment in time. Luckily, you will find the child in question open to your ideas and suggestions and, above all else, ready to take on board your wise and sensible advice.

TUESDAY 19th The Sun today lines up in a beautiful aspect with Uranus. This is likely to make for a dynamic and eventful day with probable long-term changes in both your career and inner life. Relationships are clearly emphasized and there could be a sudden attraction. Unexpected financial gains are possible and your outgoing personality will increase your ability to get the most out of life.

WEDNESDAY 20th The Moon in Leo is likely to produce minor changes in your working environment. Also, you are sure to glean some greater knowledge about somebody who has recently entered your firm. Many of you may be strongly attracted to a person who is connected with work, and this relationship will have a positive outcome.

THURSDAY 21st   The Moon in Leo makes this an ideal time for dental or medical check-ups. Not that there is likely to be much wrong with you – you seem to be in fine form and surely wish to stay that way. But remember that prevention is always better than cure.

FRIDAY 22nd   Mercury today moves into retrograde action and from our position in space appears to be going backwards. Therefore, if you have to travel or attend to paperwork over the next few weeks you are advised to double-check all arrangements, otherwise life could be unnecessarily frustrating.

SATURDAY 23rd   Do not be surprised if you find it difficult to communicate with other people today, even on the telephone – everyone seems to be at lunch, sick, or simply unavailable. Refuse to continue hitting your head against a brick wall. You can then decide that perhaps it would be a good idea to leave your telephone conversations until another time. This evening should be used for unwinding: you are certainly going to need it.

SUNDAY 24th   The new Moon today occurs in your opposite sign of Virgo and changes made in connection with relationships are likely to be good and positive. Furthermore, if you meet new people romance could get off the launching pad in record time. Professional partnerships, too, will be good as well as profitable.

MONDAY 25th   Although this is an eventful and perhaps even a lucky time, you will need to be patient as benefits will possibly be slow in coming in. Therefore, plan long term, rather than short term. Financially, there will be chances to make a new beginning, perhaps a change of direction, though not without a certain amount of difficulty.

TUESDAY 26th　This is likely to be an exceptionally hard-working day, and although you have abundant vitality, it is not easy to control. But at least your health will be good and you will not tire or run out of steam. This evening, something will occur which will affect your life and make this a period to be long remembered.

WEDNESDAY 27th　The Moon in Libra suggests you may be hearing from an official source and this may fill you with horror. However, do not jump the gun or anticipate the worst; continue to think positively and you will discover that you will be able to influence the tide of events in your favour. This evening you will need time to unwind and relax.

THURSDAY 28th　It is likely that you are being too idealistic where work matters are concerned. Others simply cannot live up to your high expectations and in order to avoid disappointment perhaps you should try to be a little bit more realistic. This evening, get as far away as possible from familiar surroundings: the further you travel the more stimulated you will be.

FRIDAY 29th　The Moon today enters into the sign of Sagittarius at the zenith of your chart. This is likely to bring interesting and positive changes as well as opportunities to improve your lifestyle. Invitations from a professional source should be accepted, and combining business with pleasure will certainly prove to be profitable.

SATURDAY 30th   Today Mercury lines up in a beautiful aspect with Venus and this tends to suggest that everyone in your life, both at work and at home, will be in a charming, romantic, helpful and humorous frame of mind. Clearly, then, if you need any favours, this is the time to ask. Many a fish will be deciding to make a special emotional commitment on this particular day.

OCTOBER

SUNDAY 1st   Although this is Sunday, your mind is very much on professional matters. You may need to fight hard to change the emphasis of your thoughts, otherwise relatives or loved ones could be feeling shut out and neglected. If you can, involve them in your plans and schemes for the future and in that way you will make them feel more important.

MONDAY 2nd   The Moon today moves into the sign of Capricorn and the emphasis will be on friends, acquaintances and fresh ambitions. There is a possibility that an older person may be handing out good advice: on reflection you will realize that you have been receiving pearls of wisdom and should perhaps take them more seriously. Avoid any independent moves for the time being.

TUESDAY 3rd   Someone you have not seen for some while is likely to be getting in touch with some interesting news or gossip. If you have been feeling isolated recently you will find this a wonderful day for getting closer to other people, relaxing and generally boosting your flagging morale. This will not be hard to do as long as you are selective.

WEDNESDAY 4th   A wonderful aspect between the Sun and Jupiter is likely to prove extremely beneficial, especially where your ambitions and finances are concerned. You are full of confidence and this will prove attractive to the opposite sex. Finance as well as social life will prosper under this useful planetary line-up. However, do not allow over-confidence to lead you into reckless spending.

THURSDAY 5th   Your ruling planet Neptune finally resumes direct movement, which means your progress will be a great deal faster and more exciting than it has been for quite some time. Wherever you have felt blocked or frustrated, you can now break free and go after your dreams in a real, positive and practical way.

FRIDAY 6th   Today Uranus joins Neptune in direct movement. From now on you will find it much easier to realize your secret hopes and wishes, although you may need to do so in conjunction with the more practical sides to life. Providing they can be made to work hand in hand, there is nothing in this life you cannot achieve – all you have to do is have faith.

SATURDAY 7th   Progressive Mars lines up with plodding Saturn, and because of this there is likely to be a stop/go feel the today. However, at least where finances are concerned, you seem to be gleaning value for money and are disinclined to throw away your hard-earned cash on frivolous items or unnecessary, expensive entertainments. Listen to the advice of an older person, too; they really know what they are talking about.

SUNDAY 8th   Today the full Moon occurs in the cash area of life and it is therefore important that you hang on to your possessions, particularly in crowds. Apart from this there is little for you to worry about: be a little more observant and you should avoid any kind of difficulty whatsoever. You may also find you are suffering from confused feelings, but the full Moon is not the best time for making efforts to understand things.

MONDAY 9th The Moon continues in the sign of Aries, creating a certain amount of fluctuation where finances are concerned. However, it is likely that you can afford to cover your expenses and there may even be opportunities to swell the family coffers today. Despite this, ensure that you give any opportunities a great deal of thought before you reach any kind of conclusion.

TUESDAY 10th Venus today enters the sign of Scorpio. This will certainly throw a rosy glow over legal matters, foreign affairs and long-distance travel. Many a fish will be attracted to those who have been swimming in very different oceans. Certainly, you are attracted to members of the opposite sex who come from completely different backgrounds. Never mind, this will titillate your sense of adventure.

WEDNESDAY 11th Your ruling planet Neptune lines up with sexy, passionate and aggressive Mars, making you much more positive in your views and where action is concerned. Right now you believe you know best, and you are right. Therefore, push ahead with anything and everyone who is important to you. A wonderful day for the sporting Piscean.

THURSDAY 12th The Moon changes sign and moves into Taurus, gingering you up physically as well as mentally. Be alert to changes that are taking place in your immediate environment as they will indicate which area of life requires your attention at this moment in time. Pay attention to phone calls, too, and return all calls or you could miss out on an opportunity and then have cause for regret.

FRIDAY 13th The Moon today enters the sign of Gemini and seems to suggest minor movements and changes in connection with family or property affairs. If you are at home you are going to be rushed off your feet, highly stimulated by everything that is happening. If you are entertaining this evening you can be sure that your guests will feel welcome, and you will be storing up a great deal of gratitude and friendship for the future.

SATURDAY 14th Today Mercury finally sees sense and resumes forward movement. Therefore, from now on your relationships in all areas should be running along well-oiled tracks. A good couple of weeks ahead for those who need to travel or deal with people involved in education or foreign affairs. You seem to be feeling much more positive and energetic at the moment.

SUNDAY 15th Aggressive Mars lines up with unexpected Uranus, producing a very lively feel to the day. You must be ready to take advantage of existing conditions, for at the moment you could charm the ugliest vultures from the trees and the slimiest snake from the grass. Use this period for furthering all of your ambitions, no matter what they may be.

MONDAY 16th The Moon today moves into the watery sign of Cancer, and this will provide you with a couple of days for really relaxing, enjoying yourself and even pursuing romance. A good day, too, for changes you need to make to creative work. Socially, life is picking up and you are spoilt for choice. All this action is sure to give your confidence a shot in the arm.

TUESDAY 17th You may be tempted to take on more responsibilities right now, especially if financial gains seem to be in the offing. Do try to be satisfied with your achievements and resist the temptation to keep on striving for more. Be sure that you go out this evening as the stars are insisting that you relax and have fun. Romance is in the air.

WEDNESDAY 18th It looks as if your friends realize that this is a decisive phase at work and that you now need a great deal of support if you are to be triumphant. Follow their advice and act upon it because this is a great time for implementing strategic and carefully-planned moves. Your love life will compensate for these difficulties, so put it all behind you and concentrate on the future.

THURSDAY 19th As Mars is in an explosive mood with Pluto today, you would be most unwise to rashly commit yourself to any kind of investments. Certainly, it is a wonderful day for considering such a move, but action should be shelved for the time being. Try to remain courteous in the company of strangers or acquaintances: you may give the unfortunate impression of arrogance, which is, of course, totally alien to your sign.

FRIDAY 20th The Sun is in a beautiful aspect to Mercury today and wherever you travel you will meet confident, optimistic and smiling faces. Even if your own mood is a little gloomy it will not take you long to brighten up and remember that you have a great deal going for you – and you are right. This can also be an important evening in your romantic life, so get out and about.

SATURDAY 21st Mars moves to the zenith of your chart and will certainly ginger up matters of a professional nature over the next few weeks. Ensure that you rest over the weekend as you are going to need every ounce of energy you can muster in order to push ahead with the plans you have in mind.

SUNDAY 22nd The Moon in your opposite sign of Virgo suggests that there may be a few surprises in store for you today. Never mind, relax: they are likely to be good and positive. Somebody may be acting out of character and this mystifies as well as intrigues you. It could be that romance is about to get off the ground.

MONDAY 23rd The Moon's placing in Libra together with other aspects seems to suggest that you are coming to the end of a long wrangle with an official source and are heaving a sigh of relief. There may even be a reason for you to celebrate and if so other people will certainly be glad to join in. If you need to air any grievances to a loved one, providing you use charm and courtesy you will be getting closer to the person who means the most to you in life.

TUESDAY 24th Today is new Moon day and it occurs in the sign of Scorpio. Although this will resurrect the idealistic side to your character, do remember that it is not always possible for other people to live up to your high ideals. By being a little bit more realistic you can avoid disappointments at a later date.

WEDNESDAY 25th Mercury lines up with Jupiter today, and it will pay you to cooperate with other people wherever necessary. Do not soldier on alone, carrying the cares of the world on your shoulders. Be prepared to delegate to those who are more than willing to extend a helping hand. All you have to do is ask – but not as easy as it sounds, particularly for a fish.

THURSDAY 26th The Sun is now fully entrenched in the sign of Scorpio and will be emphasizing everything connected with higher education, long-distance travel and foreign affairs. Many of you will decide that it is time to brush up that grey matter and this could involve a fresh course of learning. Others may form the opinion that they can benefit from a new image.

FRIDAY 27th The Moon moves into Sagittarius, the zenith point of your birth chart. Therefore, over the next couple of days there is likely to be a great deal in the way of opportunity and news on the professional front. People you meet will be useful at handing on tips, which will need to be acted upon as soon as possible. Romantically, you may develop a crush on a colleague, although the relationship may take a while to develop. Patience is required.

SATURDAY 28th Wherever you are today ensure that you keep a high profile as in this way you will attract opportunities for both fun and romance. Should you need to talk to loved ones and family, this is an ideal time for trying to sort out differences.

SUNDAY 29th The Moon today moves into the sign of Capricorn and from here on it is who you know that is really going to count. Remember, you can call in past favours if necessary and pick the brains of those you believe to be in possession of information that you desperately need. If you are at a loose end this evening why not go to a club: this is where you will find maximum fun.

MONDAY 30th These are changeable days for you. One minute you think you want one thing, the next something else. Mind you, you are not a Piscean for nothing, and indecision is part of the penalty which comes with this sign. Nevertheless, it shows your ability to be flexible and see other people's point of view – at least, that is the positive way of looking at this characteristic.

TUESDAY 31st Venus lines up in a beautiful aspect to Uranus today. This is likely to be a day which is memorable for your social life, and great, too, for all round conditions. There is also the possibility of a new dynamic relationship. Unexpected influence from other people is likely, but this element connected with the planet Uranus will be focused on your personal life. An enjoyable and pleasant day.

NOVEMBER

WEDNESDAY 1st The Sun is in a close aspect with Pluto today and this places the emphasis on cash matters and also increases the possibility that you are beginning a new phase – perhaps a complete change of direction, though not without minor difficulties. However, any challenges you experience today are only those which you are able to surmount. There may also be a tendency to clear your mind and discard old ideas.

THURSDAY 2nd Venus lines up with Pluto today and suggests you can expect a financially positive time.

Many of you may fall suddenly and deeply in love. However, the normal expression of feelings may be blocked for some reason – perhaps the other person has yet to terminate another relationship. You will be feeling passionate about literally everything today, and those who know you well may wonder what has happened to the soft and gentle Piscean they know and love.

FRIDAY 3rd Today Venus enters the zenith of your chart and will be throwing a rosy glow over professional matters. Opportunities to better yourself will come in thick and fast and it is up to you to sift the positive from the negative and prepare to take one or two minor risks. Socialize more with colleagues: you could pick up a good deal of information and may be able to finally decide in which direction you wish to go.

SATURDAY 4th Mercury moves into the sign of Scorpio, placing the emphasis on self-improvement activities as well as correspondence and documents connected with legal affairs and abroad. It is an ideal time for making long distance telephone calls; you should have little difficulty in making connections. New acquaintances who cross your path will be informative.

SUNDAY 5th For some reason you will find yourself thinking about financial matters when you would far rather turn your attention elsewhere. This may be due to the fact that you are trying to reach a decision and are suffering from your usual indecisiveness. Think long and hard before coming down on one side or the other, and stick to it. It is the only way to proceed.

MONDAY 6th The Moon in Taurus is likely to be stirring up unnecessary nervous activity. You should accomplish a great deal today if you can get your thoughts into some kind of coherent form and organize your day accordingly. As you could tend to be a little absent-minded, keep a pen and pad handy, particularly when answering the telephone.

TUESDAY 7th It is full Moon today and it occurs in the sign of Taurus. You seem to have been thinking long and hard about some change you need to make and the answer could come to you out of the blue. By all means lay down plans, but act later in the month, preferably on one of the better days.

WEDNESDAY 8th This is an especially good time for paying visits of a personal or professional nature. You will glean much in the way of insight from the encounters you make along the way. If you are searching for work you should be creating the right impression and are likely to be successful providing you think positively.

THURSDAY 9th The Moon moves into Gemini and the emphasis shifts to the personal side of life, including the family. Matters at home seem to be in a state of flux, and somebody needs to take the initiative. This is not a commodity normally associated with your sign, but even you are becoming heartily sick of all this shilly-shallying and want to bring matters to a head.

FRIDAY 10th You are likely to be in a sociable mood, but will not want to stray far from base. Therefore, it is an ideal time for asking a few friends around for a drink or a meal. They will appreciate your lively mood and enjoy your hospitality. It seems, too, that a member of the family who lives at a distance needs some kind of help and you are considering ways in which you may be able to assist.

SATURDAY 11th Today Pluto finally shakes free of Scorpio and moves into the sign of Sagittarius, where it will stay for many a year. This is a positive placing and from now on the world will slowly become a more habitable place. Mankind has left his teen years behind and finally reached maturity, becoming more responsible towards other people and not quite so wrapped up in his own selfish desires. As a self-sacrificing Piscean, this is a certainly a trend you can appreciate.

SUNDAY 12th The Moon today moves into the sign of Cancer and puts a spring in your step and a twinkle in your eye. You will certainly be in good company and could be flirting outrageously, regardless of the fact that you may be married. Luckily, those who know you well understand that you are simply testing your powers of attraction in order to assure yourself that they still exist – and of course they do.

MONDAY 13th An especially good day for attending to creative work. Everything you concern yourself with will be given that extra touch of magic that only you can create. Other people are sure to be appreciative. Certainly a good evening if you are fancy-free: get out and about, perhaps in the company of good friends who share your quirky sense of humour.

TUESDAY 14th The Moon in Leo is an indication that you are happily giving of your time, energy and services to somebody who badly needs them. Right now you may have temporarily lost your direction on the professional front, but try not to worry about this as the way ahead will soon be clear.

WEDNESDAY 15th Today Mercury is in aspect with sensible, objective Saturn, and you are able to make the decisions needed to further your ambitions, both in your professional and personal life. Don't allow yourself to be deflected by the opinions of other people: you know what is right for you, and that is all you need to know at this moment in time. This may seem selfish but you cannot constantly consider whether or not you are pleasing other people.

THURSDAY 16th Mars is in a beautiful aspect with Jupiter today and this will make you feel a great deal more optimistic about the financial side to life. There is likely to be an interesting offer for you to consider, or perhaps it is simply a case of your imagination coming to the rescue with a foolproof idea which will guarantee future security. Do not allow yourself to be bullied from your chosen path.

FRIDAY 17th The Moon today is in your opposite sign of Virgo. Those closest to you are at their most changeable, but luckily you seem to be able to adapt to their moods and desires. However, in doing so, do not overlook your own needs. Your willingness to give is admirable, but a tendency to 'cave in' under pressure can only lead to being taken for granted – be strong.

SATURDAY 18th The Moon today occupies the sign of Libra and you are seriously beginning to wonder whether or not you wish to perpetuate a current relationship. Avoid making decision today; wait a little longer and if your feelings have not changed it could be that you are wasting your time. Unless you can be sure of somebody else's devotion and commitment you could be setting yourself up to be hurt.

SUNDAY 19th Today you need stimulating company in order to lift your spirits and take you out of yourself.

Try to be as adventurous as possible, visit different places, meet new faces, and take on board the aspirations of other people: they may help you to shed light on your own life and you could gain from their past experiences.

MONDAY 20th Today Saturn resumes direct movement. Therefore, where friends have been illusive and difficult to contact, the trend now reverses and you seem to be in great demand. One of your oldest friends will pass on information which you can use in your professional life. Further, although your tolerance may be severely tested by a member of the family, eventually they will learn to respect the current stand you are making.

TUESDAY 21st Today there is a beautiful aspect between Venus and Mars: you are filled with good intentions, positive thinking and an optimistic approach to all problems. There is little you cannot achieve now that you are in this positive frame of mind. Financial problems can be solved with a bit of creative thinking. Try a fresh approach to long-standing problems and sweep them to one side.

WEDNESDAY 22nd Today there is a new Moon and it is an excellent time for making fresh starts or travelling long distances. If you have a special person abroad they are likely to get in touch, much to your delight. Many of you will experience a need to brush up your image, and should you choose to do so this will certainly boost your ego – something that should always be encouraged in members of your sign.

THURSDAY 23rd The Sun today moves into the zenith of your chart, the area of life devoted to ambitions and work. For a couple of weeks you will be striving towards a particular goal, and in the process may be neglecting those closest to you. However, if you explain your master plan they will be backing you 100 per cent.

FRIDAY 24th Today Mercury joins the Sun at the zenith of your chart making this a particularly lucky time if you travel professionally or are involved in the literary world, advertising or the media. All minor adjustments to ambitions can be useful as they will help to light your path and once this is fully illuminated you can blaze a trail straight to the top.

SATURDAY 25th The Moon in Capricorn suggests a strong need for the company of other people. You may fulfil this by visiting a club or seeking the company of friends who live close by. Should you be involved in any kind of team work, particularly of a sporting nature, you can expect to find success. Romance is fairly well starred providing you are not looking for that illusive soul mate.

SUNDAY 26th This continues to be an extremely social weekend. Your laughter, smile and personality will light up any room that you enter. Not surprisingly, you are likely to draw the attention of the opposite sex and a new romance may get off the ground. Someone in the family could be taking you for granted, and at some time soon you will have to put your foot down.

MONDAY 27th The Moon changes sign and moves into Aquarius and a contemplative and reflective mood descends. Certainly, a good time for assessing your current position in life, and how you want to proceed. However, avoid acting on impulse or it may be necessary to retrace your steps at a later date. It may help you to put down in black and white what you want out of life.

TUESDAY 28th Venus today moves into the sign of Capricorn and will be throwing a harmonious and social glow over your friendship circle. Over the next few weeks you will be inundated with invitations, and some of the occasions you attend are likely to offer chances of romance. Where there was once muddle and confusion, you now begin to see the light – and will soon be rushing towards it in an optimistic and positive way.

WEDNESDAY 29th The Moon today enters your sign and you should ensure that you stay in the limelight, both at work and when socializing. Your sense of humour will be evident and will draw the opposite sex to you. Seldom have you enjoyed so much attention.

THURSDAY 30th This is still very much a time for pushing ahead with what you want out of life, particularly if your ambitions are either creative or emotional. You won't have any difficulty in attracting the attention of those you desire, of people who can be useful to you in the near future.

DECEMBER

FRIDAY 1st The month begins with the Moon in Aries, careering through the cash area of life. Money seems to be the cause of most problems at this time and it might be a good idea to put on a brave face and confront the recent damage you may have wrought on that bank account of yours. Only when you are in full possession of the facts can you decide what needs to be done – and this will need to be done quickly.

SATURDAY 2nd   It appears that you are still attempting to balance the books. If you have allowed yourself to become panic-stricken in this area, it would be a good idea to call on the services of a friend with a sensible and cool head who can offer assurance as well as practical advice. If the worst comes to the worst you can always visit your bank manager, who will be far more welcoming than you could have envisaged. This evening opt for simple home entertainment – it will be the company that counts.

SUNDAY 3rd   The Moon today moves on into the sign of Taurus and this will enliven your whole personality. It won't be a good idea to concentrate too much on detail at work as your mind will have a tendency to wander. Shelve this for the time being and turn your attention wherever possible to being creative. Jot down original ideas that form in your head as you may be able to use them at a later date. Because of your modesty you rarely imagine that one of your inspirations could be pure gold.

MONDAY 4th   A good time for some personal shopping or bargain hunting. However, keep a tight rein on extravagance; work out exactly how much money you can afford to spend and do not go over the top, no matter how seriously you are tempted. This evening will be a perfect time for dropping in on neighbours and friends who live close by. They could make interesting introductions.

TUESDAY 5th   Today you are far more practical, rational and realistic than usual – words that are hardly ever used to describe you. Because of this you need to utilize this time well before it evaporates. Finally make up your mind over an intensely personal matter, and refuse to be 'turned around' by even the most persuasive of people. Right now you are the one who knows what is right.

WEDNESDAY 6th The Moon today moves into the sign of Gemini and is likely to bring a good deal of activity and news in connection with the family. If you are spending time at home there will be a strong desire to beautify your surroundings, and your loved ones will be delighted when they arrive home later on. Should you be at work, you will be pleasing other people with the little kindnesses that only a Piscean knows how to bestow. Just for once it looks as if you are being fully appreciated.

THURSDAY 7th Today is the time of the full Moon, and it could bring to the surface hidden feelings within the family. This could come as something of a surprise, but luckily you are adaptable and are hardly likely to be 'rocked on your heels'. Once you have gathered your wits you will be able to adapt to a fresh set of circumstances and take it from there. A good time for sitting down with someone special and making plans for the future, though not the time to act.

FRIDAY 8th Mercury is in a beautiful aspect with Jupiter and wherever you go you will find others are lucky for you. You are one of the most cooperative signs of the zodiac and if you work in harness today you are likely to reap a great deal of satisfaction, happiness and future reward. Romance is particularly well starred this evening and a relationship could really be going somewhere.

SATURDAY 9th Today it seems certain that you will enjoy the attention you deserve, and any improvement in earnings will surely be appreciated. But there is no guarantee that partners will join in the applause – far from it. Possibly they are envious or jealous, but you should refuse to be rattled or provoked into any kind of dispute. Enjoy your good fortune, you deserve it.

SUNDAY 10th You are certainly entitled to some praise and acknowledgement for the recent efforts you have put in on behalf of other people. In a personal relationship you need to make a conscious effort to be passionate and understanding – someone close may be acting out of character because they are suffering from stress. See what you can do to help them relax.

MONDAY 11th Venus is in a beautiful aspect to Saturn today and this will tend to steady those changeable emotions of yours. Furthermore, there may be some constructive financial gain and this would be an excellent time for putting financial affairs on a more reliable basis. It might be helpful for you to discuss these matters with someone older or more experienced. You don't have to act on their suggestions, but it would be worth giving them a hearing.

TUESDAY 12th Mercury today moves into the sign of Capricorn, and because of this it is a 'newsy' kind of day. However, you must learn to separate information from tittle-tattle and gossip otherwise you may be misled. Somewhere inside most Pisceans is a sensible person struggling to get out, and today is the time for setting that person free.

WEDNESDAY 13th The Moon in Virgo suggests that although you may be relying on the assistance of somebody else, due to circumstances beyond their control they may be unable to fulfil their side of the bargain.

Although you won't, of course, become vindictive, you may feel hurt inside. Do not blow this matter out of all proportion.

THURSDAY 14th You seem to be consorting with a lot of new faces today and finding their company stimulating. But at work and in your social life this evening you are drawn to those who come from completely different backgrounds or cultures. You appear to be consciously trying to broaden your horizons. A good move for any sign of the zodiac.

FRIDAY 15th Someone on whom you were relying may let you down today. This is not intentional and you should not take it to heart. The credit side of this situation is that it now starts to prove just how independent and practical you can be if you put your mind to it. Isn't that so? The answer to this question is definitely 'yes'.

SATURDAY 16th As Venus is in beautiful aspect to your ruling planet Neptune, you are at your most creative and dreamy, and it is best to set aside practical issues for the time being and give free rein to that Piscean spirit. You will be easily charmed by the opposite sex, and it is imperative that you avoid taking yourself too seriously until you have plucked up the courage to remove those rose-tinted glasses. But there's no need to do so immediately, enjoy your trip if only for one day. Good constructive work can be accomplished under such a favourable aspect.

SUNDAY 17th Today the Moon enters the sign of Libra and, like it or not, it is time to retrace your steps and pick up unfinished work in order to complete it. Whatever you do, do not leave a trail of half-baked ideas or chores; ensure that you complete everything that you set out to do. In this way others may realize that it is possible to rely on a Piscean.

MONDAY 18th The Moon today enters the watery sign of Scorpio, boosting your confidence, lifting your spirits and resurrecting the adventurous and sociable side to your character. An ideal time for approaching people who perhaps on occasions tend to intimidate you. Today it will take a brave man or woman to throw you off course.

TUESDAY 19th The Sun is in a beautiful aspect to Jupiter, and it is one of those days when what Pisces wants 'Pisces gets'. All you have to do is decide exactly what that is. On the work front you will be making useful contacts by mixing business with pleasure, and they will prove to be invaluable at a later date. Step out of the shadows, and strike out into life: now is the time for bold, courageous moves.

WEDNESDAY 20th Venus and Uranus are in beautiful aspect, and because of this today may be marked by memorable, sociable and good all round conditions. Interesting ties of affection are likely to be formed – the time is right for change and you must push ahead. There is a strong possibility, too, that a powerful influence in your life seems to be taking up the majority of your time, attention and affection. Could it be love? Yes, it most certainly could.

THURSDAY 21st Although the Moon is at the zenith of your chart, placing the emphasis on career matters, it is unlikely that you will achieve a great deal. There seems to be a certain amount of disruption at work, though in the pleasantest of ways. Other people are in top form and because of this you may be combining business with pleasure. It might be a good idea to remain sober while doing so. See what you can do.

FRIDAY 22nd The new Moon today occurs at the zenith of your chart, suggesting that any changes you want to put into operation on the professional front are well starred. As always with the new Moon, it is an excellent time for meeting people and generally being more adventurous. Be prepared to step outside your usual circle when socializing this evening. You need plenty of stimulation today – go where you can find it.

SATURDAY 23rd Today Venus moves into Aquarius and over the next couple of weeks you could find yourself involved in a relationship which requires secrecy. As a sensitive, loyal and emotional fish, this is not the most desirable of situations for you, and where possible you should strive strenuously to avoid it. Be open and honest where your emotional life is concerned and you will end this year full of joy and optimism rather than regret.

SUNDAY 24th Mercury is in strong aspect to sexy, aggressive Mars. Consequently, you could find that other people are making some heavy demands on your time and energy, which could make for a highly-charged sexual day. Alternatively, you may be foolish enough to allow yourself to be constantly at the beck and call of other people. If so, at some point it will be necessary for you to put your foot down. The days when you were afraid to say no to others have long passed.

MONDAY 25th You seem to be enjoying yourself in a rather quiet way. There is a distinct possibility that you may have run out of energy: if so, feel free to relax and allow everybody else to participate in all the celebrations going on whilst you recuperate, replenish and recharge. Tomorrow is another day, and one which you fully intend to enjoy.

TUESDAY 26th Today the Moon is in your sign and you are keeping a high profile. If anybody is going to be the life and soul of any gathering it is you. You are equally at ease with young children and octogenarians: you find it 'easy to walk a mile in other people's shoes' and can understand exactly how they feel in any given circumstance. The love you give is sure to be well received, perhaps because you are not expecting anything in return.

WEDNESDAY 27th Other people seem to be flagging and it may be up to you to generate some excitement as well as movement. Luckily, you are full of energy. Where possible you should get in contact with nature, if only for an hour. This will help to blow away the cobwebs from not only yourself but your family and loved ones. You will then be ready to participate in a social occasion this evening.

THURSDAY 28th A beautiful aspect between Mercury and your ruling planet Neptune could have quite an effect on you. You are likely to be more flexible, vibrant and full of good ideas, and inevitably others will be drawn to your magnetism and charisma. It is a great day for asking for favours, and a time when romance could occupy a great deal of your time. If you are single you may well meet someone important and, if so, this relationship is likely to be long lasting. Be sure that you make the most of your time.

FRIDAY 29th The Moon enters the sign of Aries and you may be tempted to rush out and spend money you can ill afford. Should you feel there is a strong possibility of this happening, send other people out on errands while you stay at home. Fortunately the shops need to close at some time and it is then you can emerge and visit friends who live close by. You will need stimulating companionship as at present you are consumed with a new hobby or pastime and wish to discuss it with other people.

SATURDAY 30th   Mars is in a wonderful aspect with your ruling planet Neptune. This will increase your energy levels, your sex appeal and your ability to take the initiative. Just for once you will be toppling Aries and Leo from their dominant position and taking over. Don't be surprised if you are surrounded by shocked faces. There is a possibility, too, of your receiving a late present which delights you. Right now you are full of optimism for the year on the horizon, though at the same time feeling fairly sentimental about 1995, which on the whole has been a good year for you.

SUNDAY 31st   Mercury is in close aspect with unexpected and eccentric Uranus today, and this is the frame of mind you will find in those closest to you. Others are springing surprises and there is never a dull moment. You seem to have various options on how to spend your leisure time this evening. Choose that which seems to offer the most in the way of adventure and excitement: new attractions are likely to spring up and take you by surprise. What a wonderful way to end any year.

HAPPY NEW YEAR

Moon Tables

THE MOON AND YOUR MOODS

Our moods and, indeed, the strength of our intuition are clearly affected by the Moon. After all, you may ask yourself on occasions, why on earth does such a well-balanced person as me suddenly become bad-tempered, frigid, emotional or sentimental on certain days. Well, I'm afraid it is all down to the position of the Moon. Why not try an experiment, and attempt to prove it to yourself?

Glance at the Moon table for any given week or month and then put it away. In the meantime, in your diary make notes of your moods and reactions to situations. Once this period has expired, rescue your book, turn to the Moon tables and you will notice a clear pattern of behaviour developing. You don't need an astrologer to work out for you that, during the week, or during the period whilst you were taking notes, the Moon was, for example, in Scorpio when you were feeling depressed, in Cancer, maybe, when you were feeling romantic and Aries when you developed headaches and were bad-tempered, etc.

Your own individual pattern is likely to be repeated monthly. However, do not give in or be surprised if you are unaffected when the Moon passes through certain signs. It may be, for example, that whilst it made its way through Aries and Libra, you were neither elated nor depressed. What does this mean? Well, such a happening would merely suggest that these two signs are not particularly prominent on your own individual birthchart.

Female readers will probably like to take note of the fact that very often their menstrual cycle, if of normal length, will begin when the Moon is in the same one or two signs, each month. Why not be a devil and experiment? Give it a try. You have nothing to lose and after all you may find out an awful lot about yourself.

FULL AND NEW MOONS FOR 1995

January	1st New in ♑	16th Full in ♋	30th New in ♒
February	15th Full in ♌		
March	1st New in ♓	17th Full in ♍	31st New in ♈
April	15th Full in ♎	29th New in ♉	
May	14th Full in ♏	29th New in ♊	
June	13th Full in ♐	28th New in ♋	
July	12th Full in ♑	27th New in ♌	
August	10th Full in ♒	26th New in ♍	
September	9th Full in ♓	24th New in ♏	
October	8th Full in ♈	24th New in ♏	
November	7th Full in ♉	22nd New in ♏	
December	7th Full in ♊	22nd New in ♐	

KEY

♈ Aries	♌ Leo	♐ Sagittarius
♉ Taurus	♍ Virgo	♑ Capricorn
♊ Gemini	♎ Libra	♒ Aquarius
♋ Cancer	♏ Scorpio	♓ Pisces

FULL AND NEW MOONS FOR 1995

Jan	Feb	Mar	Apr	May	Jun	Jul	Aug	Sept	Oct	Nov	Dec	
♑	♓	♓	♈	♊	♋	♌	♎	♏	♑	♒	♈	1
♑	♓	♓	♉	♊	♋	♍	♎	♐	♑	♓	♈	2
♒	♓	♈	♉	♊	♌	♍	♏	♐	♒	♓	♉	3
♒	♈	♈	♊	♋	♌	♍	♏	♑	♒	♈	♉	4
♓	♈	♉	♊	♋	♍	♎	♐	♑	♓	♈	♉	5
♓	♉	♉	♊	♋	♍	♎	♐	♎	♓	♉	♊	6
♈	♉	♉	♋	♌	♍	♏	♐	♎	♓	♉	♊	7
♈	♉	♊	♋	♌	♎	♏	♑	♓	♈	♉	♋	8
♈	♊	♊	♌	♍	♎	♐	♑	♓	♈	♊	♋	9
♉	♊	♋	♌	♍	♏	♐	♒	♈	♉	♊	♋	10
♉	♋	♋	♌	♎	♏	♑	♒	♈	♉	♋	♌	11
♊	♋	♋	♍	♎	♐	♑	♓	♉	♊	♋	♌	12
♊	♌	♌	♍	♏	♐	♒	♓	♉	♊	♋	♍	13
♊	♌	♌	♎	♏	♑	♒	♈	♉	♊	♌	♍	14
♋	♌	♍	♎	♐	♑	♓	♈	♊	♋	♌	♍	15
♋	♍	♍	♏	♐	♒	♓	♉	♊	♋	♍	♎	16
♌	♍	♎	♏	♑	♒	♈	♉	♋	♌	♍	♎	17
♌	♎	♎	♐	♑	♓	♈	♉	♋	♌	♎	♏	18
♍	♎	♏	♐	♒	♓	♈	♊	♋	♌	♎	♏	19
♍	♏	♏	♑	♒	♈	♉	♊	♌	♍	♎	♐	20
♍	♏	♏	♑	♓	♈	♉	♋	♌	♍	♏	♐	21
♎	♐	♐	♒	♓	♉	♊	♋	♍	♎	♏	♑	22
♎	♐	♐	♒	♓	♉	♊	♋	♍	♎	♐	♑	23
♏	♑	♑	♓	♈	♉	♊	♌	♍	♏	♐	♒	24
♏	♑	♑	♓	♈	♊	♋	♌	♎	♏	♑	♒	25
♐	♑	♒	♓	♉	♊	♋	♍	♎	♐	♑	♓	26
♐	♒	♒	♈	♉	♊	♌	♍	♏	♐	♒	♓	27
♑	♒	♓	♈	♉	♋	♌	♎	♏	♑	♒	♈	28
♑		♓	♉	♊	♋	♌	♎	♐	♑	♓	♈	29
♒		♈	♉	♊	♌	♎	♎	♐	♒	♓	♈	30
♒		♈		♋		♍	♏		♒		♉	31